To mel

DEADLY
ODDS

Great chatting with
you. Hope you
enjoy the book.

Look forward to
meeting you!

Sincerely
mike
Barbahu

RECOVERY FROM COMPULSIVE GAMBLING

DEADLY
ODDS

RECOVERY FROM COMPULSIVE GAMBLING

KEN ESTES and MIKE BRUBAKER

Affiliated Writers of America, Inc. / Publishers
Encampment, Wyoming

Affiliated Writers of America, Inc. / Publishers
P.O. Box 343
Encampment, Wyoming 82325
307-327-5328

Trade Softcover Edition
ISBN: 1-879915-82-0

PUBLISHING HISTORY

Fireside/Parkside Paperback Edition: 1994
Published by Simon and Schuster

CONTENTS

THE BIG WIN

O n a fall night in 1986, Alex Petros entered a realm most gamblers only dream about. Late that night, he began a fantastic run at a blackjack table at the lavish Caesars Tahoe Casino in South Lake Tahoe, Nevada. Four hours later he walked away from the table a $650,000 winner.

During those four hours, the world had stood still for Alex Petros. He had been consumed by a magic that had all but blotted out everything around him in the bustling, noisy casino. He was aware only of his heart pounding and the sound of his own voice amidst the blur of cards, chips, and money on the green felt of the seven-slot blackjack table. He played with a profound sense of exhilaration. He had never before felt so powerful. And he has never felt so powerful since.

FLIGHTS OF FANCY AND TROUBLING UNDERCURRENTS

Alex hadn't planned a trip to Tahoe that night. The impulse had hit him after he had found himself home alone in his hillside home in a fashionable section of San Francisco overlooking the Pacific Ocean. Usually Alex was on the go, hopping from one restaurant, bar, or nightspot to another with his girlfriend in tow. On that night in October, however, his girlfriend, Julie, was in Sacramento visiting relatives. Alex was bored.

Alex, a thirty-six-year-old San Franciscan of Greek descent, was bored a lot. Usually, though, he could find relief in booze, a few snorts of cocaine, or a trip to Europe, Africa, or some other exotic place. And, of course, there was always gambling.

Alex could easily afford these flights of fancy. In 1980, he received $9 million for his share of some investment holdings his family had sold. From the age of four, he had been living off the bounty of an inheritance from his father who had amassed great wealth in shipping and other ventures. As an adult, Alex owned an apartment house valued at $2 million that brought in $9,000 a month in rent; he had funds from the sale four years earlier of two upscale San Francisco restaurants that he had owned and operated; and he had another small fortune in stocks and bonds.

In his thirty-six years, Alex had never held a real job. His restaurant venture was almost a real job, but he left the day-to-day operation of the restaurants to others. He was content to act primarily as the bon vivant host of the establishments.

Alex had been footloose in his youth and had bounced around from school to school, attending a series of private schools in the San Francisco Bay Area, a military academy, and then a succession of universities—the last of which was in Europe. The only reason he tolerated college was to maintain his draft deferment.

Alex Petros was a playboy. He had both money and time to burn. He burned them freely, much to the distress of his seventy-year-old mother and his brother, who knew that Alex's life was a charade that would someday fall apart.

Alex was frequently depressed. He experienced dark undercurrents of self-doubt, inadequacy, and guilt stemming from his early childhood. Alex was not born into wealth. When he was three years old in his native Greece, his widowed father had put him and his brother up for adoption. Alex's natural mother died while giving birth to Alex, and he later learned that his natural father had died in Greece at the age of forty-one of what Alex suspects was chronic alcoholism. He has no conscious recall of his early childhood in Greece, but frequently he is haunted by dreams that he feels are rooted in his childhood.

INSTANT GRATIFICATION

Alex is a tall, slender man with a swarthy complexion, a neatly trimmed mustache, a luxuriant shock of gray-flecked black hair, and a friendly, engaging manner. He is extremely generous with his friends but notes with a laugh that he's even more generous with himself. He was spoiled as a child and is incredibly self-indulgent, which is apparent from his life-style. He has the best of everything in his kitchen appliances, his artwork, his home, and his fleet of expensive foreign automobiles. Like any self-indulgent person, when Alex wants something, he wants it immediately. When he found himself alone and bored on that Friday night in 1986, he quickly decided to seek instant gratification in gambling. Gambling was exciting.

He sometimes gambled in the card clubs of San Francisco, but this time he wanted more excitement than the clubs could offer. So he took a couple of snorts of cocaine and at eight o'clock, he climbed into his 1980 Rolls-Royce, bound for Caesars Tahoe some two hundred miles northeast of San Francisco.

Caesars Tahoe is a magnificent 450-room, 15-story hotel and casino on the southern banks of Lake Tahoe, the eastern shore of which forms the border between California and Nevada. Patrons, casino workers, and residents of the Lake Tahoe area like to think of their area as a world apart from the Nevada gambling mecca of Las Vegas four hundred miles to the south. They regard Las Vegas as garish and seedy. The two settings are certainly a world apart. Tahoe is located in the pristine High Sierras of California and Nevada at an elevation of over 6,000 feet, and in the winter the area resembles the cover of a Christmas card with majestic snow-covered pines towering over the dark blue lake. Las Vegas, however, is about as far from serenity and nature as anyone could imagine, with colorful neon signs perched atop gigantic 3,000-room hotels and casinos in the arid high desert country east of Los Angeles.

The difference between Tahoe and Las Vegas is reflected in Caesars operations in the two areas. Caesars Tahoe is less than a third of the size of its glitzy Las Vegas cousin, Caesars Palace, and promotes ski packages and beach outings for its guests.

The scenery and the nongambling activities of Tahoe, however, held no allure for Alex Petros. The trip from his front door to the blackjack table at Caesars Tahoe had taken him three and a half hours. His boredom had vanished the minute he slid behind the wheel of his Rolls-Royce. It was overwhelmed by the rush of excitement that had been building in intensity as he drew near the Nevada state line.

Alex Petros was no stranger to Caesars Tahoe or for that matter to Caesars Palace in Las Vegas. Moreover, he was personally acquainted with the casino manager, a man whom he referred to as the "big boss." He thought the casino manager was a "nice person."

Alex had a relatively modest $10,000 line of credit at Caesars, but the casino knew he was good for more. They had routinely checked out Alex's finances when he applied for his credit line and they were undoubtedly pleased with what they saw. Alex usually paid his gambling debts with the casino within seven days, which also pleased management. Later, Alex's credit line would be extended to $50,000, and the casino would gladly raise it to $100,000, $150,000, or more on Alex's request. In fact, Alex thought at times that the casino was too generous with its credit. "They really should stop you at a certain point," he would say later. Alex's wins and losses at Caesars generally had matched his credit line—$5,000 to $10,000.

Alex was a progressive bettor. He'd start out with a bet of $200 and, if he was winning, push it in stages to $300, $400, $500, and so on. If he lost, he'd return to the $200 level and stay there until he started winning again. At times, though, he'd be too fatigued or too drunk to stay with his game plan and would invariably end up losing more than he had planned.

BOREDOM TRANSFORMED

Like most experienced gamblers, he played only one game seriously. His game was blackjack. After he arrived in Tahoe, Alex walked briskly to the blackjack table. On the way to Tahoe, he had mapped out a variation to his customary betting strategy. This time he would open the betting at $500 a hand and play three hands simultaneously. He found playing one hand at a time much too slow. Alex didn't feel particularly lucky or unlucky that night. He wasn't given to hunches or omens. All he wanted was action; in a way, even the money was secondary. Money was only fuel for the fire and the more money he risked, the more excitement he felt.

Alex, who rarely bet less than $100 on anything ("I wouldn't know what a five-dollar or ten-dollar bet would feel like," he says), played at the $100- to $5,000-bet table. It was the highest-stakes table in the house and Alex and other high rollers preferred it because the $100 minimum scared away casual bettors and tourists who usually clustered around the five-dollar tables. Inexperienced players slowed down the action, and nothing was going to slow down Alex on the night of his big win.

One of the high-stakes tables was empty when Alex arrived. The dealer stood impassively at the table with three decks of cards fanned out in front of him. Alex sat down at the table, motioned for the pit boss, and signed a credit slip for $5,000. The dealer counted out $5,000 in white and black chips. The whites were worth $500 each, the blacks $100. Alex plunked down $500 in each of three wager squares in front of him. The dealer shuffled the cards and then dispensed them rhythmically from the "shoe" with a crisp, snapping motion. The game was on. The boredom of four hours earlier had given way to a sensation of butterflies in Alex's stomach and a sense of anticipation.

Everything was to Alex's liking. He had the table to himself, which meant he and he alone could control the action and pace. He didn't recognize the dealer from his earlier forays to the casino, but he knew that the dealers Caesars assigned to the high-stakes tables liked action, too. When the action was fast and the stakes high, so were the tips.

The casino was abuzz with activity, which added to the feeling of excitement. He could hear the whirl of the nearby roulette wheels, the shouts, the laughter, and the groans of the players at the craps tables, and the rattle of the coins from the slot machines and the video poker machines. It was late and getting later, the time when the big gamblers venture forth. The casinos were jammed with other gamblers and flooded with crowds entering and leaving the nightclub shows. It was the gambler's bewitching hour.

Alex won consistently for the first few hands and nonchalantly exchanged the white chips for yellows, which are worth $1,000 each. He could feel the excitement rising within him. He usually won in the beginning, but shortly after he began playing that night, the thought struck him that he simply could not lose. All the cards were falling his way. He was too excited to sit, so he pushed aside the stool on which he was sitting and stood up. He was betting $1,000, $2,000, $3,000 a hand by now and was easily tens of thousands of dollars ahead.

BETTING THE LIMIT

The action, however, was still not fast enough for Alex. Even the winning had become too routine. Alex decided to accelerate the pace by playing all seven slots at the table. He also pushed his bets to the limit—$5,000 a hand or $10,000 when he would pair up and split a hand. At the first few breaks in the action, when the dealer was reshuffling the cards, Alex converted some chips to cash and by one o'clock or one thirty in the morning, the table was covered with cash and chips. Alex dipped into the cash from time to time to lavish big tips on the cocktail waitress and the dealer. He would shove $1,000 tips at the dealer, and whip out hundred-dollar bills for the waitress every time she refreshed his drink. He felt no effect from the liquor he was sipping—he was already sky-high from the gambling. "I was feeling like king of the hill," said Alex. "I just couldn't get enough." At about one o'clock, when he was nearly $200,000 ahead, Alex decided to go for it. "I was convinced I couldn't lose. I thought, 'Tonight's the night I'm finally going to get these SOBs,'" Alex recalls. He called over the pit boss, who had been standing at the end of the table monitoring the rapid exchange of cards and chips flashing in front of him. His presence was just window dressing at this point. Gamblers like Alex wouldn't risk cheating because to be caught would mean permanent exile from the casino. And dealers wouldn't risk the embarrassment of shorting a high roller like Alex and getting called on it.

High-stakes players possess an uncanny ability to keep track of their cards and bets no matter how fast the action is. "I would know in an instant if I was so much as a chip or a dollar short," Alex states. This feeling is common among players on Alex's level.

The boss responded quickly to Alex's summons and Alex asked him to raise the limit to $10,000. The boss conferred briefly with his manager and nodded his approval to Alex and the dealer. Alex quickly placed ten $1,000 chips at each of the seven slots, and the dealer once again began dispensing cards from the "shoe" to his left. Alex didn't even glance at the dealer. He was focused only on the action immediately in front of him as he ran from one end of the table to the other, checking his cards, splitting hands, and snapping off "hit" commands to the dealer. Once, he was able to split several hands, upping the stakes on the table to $120,000 for one deal. Alex won and raked in another ninety yellow chips.

The action hadn't escaped the attention of others in the bustling, dimly lit casino. Other patrons began gathering behind the table to watch Alex, which prompted the casino to dispatch security guards to cordon off the space immediately around him. Alex continued to move from one end of the table to the other with each crisp turn of the card. It was great theater.

THE NEXT ROUND OF ACTION

Lake Tahoe couldn't ask for anything better. Alex was vaguely aware of the throng that had gathered and the gasps they uttered when the dealer "busted" and mechanically covered Alex's winning hand with stacks of yellow chips. He enjoyed hearing the sounds of the crowd, because they added to his rush and his sense of control and power. He never once looked back at the crowd, as he did when he was playing in Monte Carlo or the pia gow games in the card parlors in the San Francisco Bay Area, where spectators are encouraged to bet on a player's hand. He was concentrating solely on the table, the cards, and the plotting of his next bets.

The game was moving as fast as humanly possible now and Alex's winnings were mounting. Within minutes after raising the stakes, he passed the $300,000 mark and about a half hour later, he was at $400,000. He was winning on virtually every deal. When the action periodically stopped for the dealer to reshuffle the decks, Alex suddenly felt tired and edgy, but those feelings vanished the instant play resumed.

When Alex passed the $500,000 mark and then $600,000, he was conscious of his heart racing and great bursts of energy, probably from adrenaline rushes. But at about two thirty, a feeling of exhaustion suddenly overwhelmed him. He thought the next round of action would revitalize him, but it didn't. His legs felt like lead, his concentration faltered, and he began to feel as if he was losing his edge. It was crazy, he thought, since it wasn't unusual for him to gamble all night, sometimes even around the clock. He would have liked to raise the limit again to see whether that would recharge him, but he knew it was futile to ask. Ten thousand dollars was the house's ultimate limit. So at two thirty, four hours after he began, Alex announced he was quitting.

Alex had never quit so abruptly before. Later he couldn't even explain the decision. He didn't quit to protect his winnings. He simply quit because he was bone tired and in somewhat of a daze. "It's strange," Alex recalled later, "but it seems like the high from winning doesn't last nearly as long as the high from chasing [your money] to get even. I can't explain it; that's just the way it is for me."

If the dealer and the pit boss were surprised by Alex's move, they didn't show it. They quickly moved forward to help Alex gather his chips and escorted him to the cashier's window. Although Alex was tired, he retained that feeling of power. As he left the table, he took note for the first time of the crowd that had been watching him play. He enjoyed attracting looks of awe as he made his way to the cashier. He equated the feeling to what athletes or performers must feel as they walk through a crowd of adoring fans after a good performance.

The Caesars cashier counted out 6,500 one-hundred-dollar bills, bundled them up, and placed them in a bag, which she handed to Alex. Clutching the bag containing $650,000, Alex was escorted by security guards into the hotel lobby, then to a suite high above the casino floor. As he made his way to the suite, Alex thought how funny it was that he should have a suite. In his hurry and mounting excitement, he had not even made a room reservation after arriving from San Francisco.

Exhausted, Alex made straight for the bed shortly after entering the room, but he quickly discovered that he couldn't sleep. The rush of excitement had passed and he felt alone. There was no one with whom he could share his victory. He could tell a few friends about it, but he couldn't talk about the experience with his girlfriend, his mother, or his brother. He had tried to minimize his gambling to them. He also found himself agonizing over reporting his winnings to the IRS. He wasn't particularly worried about the taxes he would owe; he was more concerned about his gambling activities showing up on his individual tax return. Earlier, when he was in the restaurant business, he had been denied a loan by a bank when the bank noticed that he had reported gambling losses on his tax return. He hadn't reported any gambling losses since then, but now he would be forced to report his winnings. If he didn't, he could be guilty of tax evasion. He thought, "Gambling's so damned stupid. You lose even when you win."

Finally, after about three hours of tossing and turning, he got out of bed, showered, dressed, and checked out of the hotel. His only luggage was the small bag containing the $650,000. Before leaving, Alex called his girlfriend at her parents' home in Sacramento and told her he would be by in a couple of hours for breakfast. Over breakfast, he told Julie he had had a good night at the tables—nothing more. After breakfast, he drove back home to San Francisco and finally dropped off to sleep. He had been gone from home about sixteen hours. Alex Petros' great run was over.

2

THE BOTTOM

Michael Clark Brubaker was making a house call. On a brilliant Saturday morning in September 1989, the fifty-year-old alcoholism counselor left his home in the village of Carmel, California, on the Monterey Peninsula and drove about two hours north to the elegant Presidio Heights area of San Francisco in response to a telephone call he had received the night before. The caller was Anna Petros, the septuagenarian matriarch of the Petros family trust. Anna Petros had told Mike that her son, Alex, had failed to meet his girlfriend and a group of friends the night before at a San Francisco nightclub and hadn't been heard from for about twenty-four hours. She was worried. She suspected Alex was off on a gambling binge.

Mike Brubaker, a one-time compulsive gambler, shared Anna Petros' suspicions. He told her not to worry; he would drive up the following morning to see what he could do to help. Mike, who had quit gambling eleven years earlier and had stopped drinking four years before that, maintained his abstinence from alcohol and gambling by helping other alcoholics and compulsive gamblers. When a

call came, even if it was Saturday morning and he was looking forward to a golf game, he responded.

Mike had never met Anna Petros. He later learned that
Mrs. Petros had gotten his telephone number from Alex's
girlfriend, Julie. She had accompanied Alex to a couple of
meetings for compulsive gamblers earlier in the summer at
the alcoholism and drug dependency treatment center in
Monterey where Mike worked.

AN UNEASY TRUCE

Mike was sure that Alex Petros was a compulsive gambler,
because he had acknowledged his problem and had vowed
that he wanted to stop gambling. In an effort to grapple
with his gambling problem, Alex bought a weekend retreat
in Carmel a few blocks from Brubaker's house in which he
could seek peace and the beginnings of a new, less frenetic
life-style. He also was seeing a psychologist in Carmel on a
regular basis, and, at the suggestion of the psychologist, he
had begun to attend self-help meetings for gamblers that
summer in Monterey. He had met Mike Brubaker at these
meetings and had taken an instant liking to Mike.

At best, though, Alex's attempts at recovery produced
an uneasy truce. He was still beset by boredom and he had
accelerated his alcohol and cocaine use in an effort to alleviate his general uneasiness, if not actual depression. For
the first time in his life, he had begun to feel squeezed for
money. Although Alex had a net worth of several million
dollars and a steady annual income of well over $100,000
from stocks, bonds, and real estate investments, he was
cash-poor from servicing gambling debts and bad investments. That meant he couldn't wing off with Julie for his
more or less quarterly jaunts to Europe, Africa, or the Far
East, or indulge his taste for expensive cars and gadgets. So
despite his expressed and apparently heartfelt desire to

stop gambling and his absence of several weeks from the gaming tables, Alex Petros was not a man at peace with himself. He was a long way from the fired-up player he had been in 1986, when he took away $650,000 from Caesars Tahoe.

As Mike Brubaker made his way up the walk to Anna Petros' rambling home overlooking San Francisco Bay, he knew the object of Anna Petros' concern was safe inside. When Mike had called a few minutes before arriving to confirm his appointment, Alex had answered the phone. Mike was greeted at the door by Mrs. Petros, a small, proper woman, and Alex's brother Tony. He thought both seemed warm, but wary. When he entered the foyer, Mike saw a somber, bleary-eyed, disheveled Alex Petros gingerly making his way down the staircase from the second floor. Alex was wearing a bathrobe and was obviously suffering from a lack of sleep. Mike thought he looked totally exhausted.

Brubaker was not surprised by Alex's appearance. During his twelve years in the alcoholism treatment field, Mike had seen a lot of men and women broken by their addictions. Still, he couldn't help but contrast the Alex Petros standing before him with the lively, engaging, well-groomed man-about-town he had seen at a meeting in Monterey only a week before. As a counselor, Mike knew this might be a golden opportunity for him to get through to Alex about his gambling and drug abuse. Alex may have hit his bottom as a compulsive gambler and finally might be ready to accept the help he so desperately needed.

QUICK SCORE GONE AWRY

About thirty hours before he greeted Mike Brubaker at the foot of the stairs in his mother's house, Alex Petros had suddenly caved in to an overpowering impulse to gamble.

He had resisted the urge to gamble several times since he had begun attending the Gamblers Anonymous meetings in Monterey, but this time it was different. Fueled by alcohol and cocaine, he began fantasizing about a big win that would get him squared away financially, and the fantasy ran away with him. He had dined with Julie and some friends at a San Francisco restaurant and even suggested that the group rendezvous at a nightclub later that night. Julie and Alex's friends showed up at the nightclub as scheduled, but Alex did not. Relinquishing himself to his compulsion, he headed to a card parlor near San Francisco International Airport immediately after dinner. He had planned to play a few high-stake hands of pia gow, a fast-paced Chinese card game, and to rejoin his friends later. He thought if he were lucky, he could make a quick score of $100,000 or more in an hour or two. He played twenty-eight straight hours and lost $110,000.

Alex Petros began to gravitate to the card clubs ringing San Francisco after a two-year run of heavy losses at the casinos in Tahoe and Las Vegas. He felt more in control of his destiny at the card clubs, where he played against other players instead of the house. The clubs were easily accessible and Alex was finding that he needed to gamble more often to cover his losses and to overcome his constant state of depression.

Alex's bad run at the casinos began shortly after his big win of $650,000 at Caesars Tahoe in 1986. That big win had merely whetted Alex's appetite for high-stakes gambling, and he had returned three weeks later to Caesars in the company of several friends. They arrived in Tahoe in style. Caesars had sent a private jet to San Francisco to pick them up and everything was on the house—rooms, food, shows, drinks, transportation.

Alex had started out on a roll at the same blackjack table on which he had won big only three weeks earlier. He was betting $5,000 each on three hands, and within a couple of hours he was up $95,000. He was king of the hill again—omnipotent.

Alex's friends implored him to quit while he was ahead, but he was too consumed by the action to stop. After losing a few hands in succession, Alex halfheartedly gave in to his friends' urging and agreed to accompany them to the nightclub show, at which Chubby Checker was performing. He thought the break in the action might end his losing streak. He couldn't wait to get back to the table, however. Immediately after the show, he rushed back to the blackjack table over his friends' protests. He didn't leave the table again until six o'clock the next morning. By then, he was $500,000 down.

THROWING IN THE TOWEL

In remembering that evening, Alex could not recall winning a single hand after going up by $95,000. "If I won, I don't remember it," he says. "All I remember is losing one hand right after another and doubling my bets to try to catch up." The action was as heavy as it had been twenty-one days earlier when Alex was winning big. Alex was on his feet, snapping off commands to the dealer. Once again, a crowd gathered to watch the action, but this time they greeted the results with shocked silence and murmurs as Alex suffered loss after loss. Finally, a subdued Alex threw in the towel, signed a note with a sympathetic pit boss for $500,000, and retreated to his room, where he slipped into his customary sense of aloneness and depression.

"I kept thinking about what I had done and how stupid I had been. I thought about Julie, my family, all the poverty in the world, how I was pissing my life away . . . everything. I was tense and shaking. I wanted to tell someone how I felt. I wanted someone to understand. But I was too ashamed to tell anyone how much I had lost."

Alex's depression lasted the rest of that day and on through the weekend, but once he worked out a plan to pay off his losses, the depression lifted slightly. He had covered much of the loss with what remained of his $650,000 winnings from three weeks earlier. He agreed to pay off the balance over a year's time, which he did. The big loss, however, hardly dimmed his enthusiasm for gambling. If anything, it heightened it. He didn't want to quit a loser and he longed to regain that feeling of power that only winning could produce.

For the next three years, Alex continued to gamble in Tahoe, Las Vegas, the Bay Area card clubs, and casinos all around the world. He also began to look for other ways to raise huge sums of cash to support his gambling and his lavish life-style. One of those ways was the commodities market. Alex took a $3 million plunge into South African gold futures following the stock market crash of 1987. He thought wary investors would forsake the stock market and invest heavily in precious metals. His speculation in gold futures was high-stakes gambling at its peak. The futures market fluctuated wildly, often as much as 15 to 20 percent in a day, and Alex would call his broker four or five times daily to buy and sell or simply verify his position.

Once on the spur of the moment, Alex decided to visit South Africa to check out his investment. Today, he laughs about the trip. "I don't know what in the hell I planned to check out. I just recall looking at the gold mines and thinking, 'I've invested millions in a big hole in the ground.' " At their peak, Alex's gold futures were worth $4.8 million, but when he sold out six months later, they were valued at only $1.6 million. "I lost big in options," Alex said later. "I loved the action, but no one can afford to play that game very long if they're losing."

Despite his big plunge into the commodities market, Alex's primary passion continued to be cards. He lost steadily, however, and was always in debt to the casinos and card clubs. His last outing at the casino prior to the September binge that prompted Alex's mother to call Mike Brubaker resulted in a $75,000 loss, and he didn't fare much better at the two card clubs where he regularly played.

Including that September binge, Alex Petros' losses from 1986 to 1989 totalled a staggering $5 million. Although not financially devastated, he was nonetheless caught on a treadmill. His losses would leave him depressed for weeks at a time and the only way he could relieve the depression was to gamble again. He began to feel he was insane. For the first time he began to think about suicide. It seemed he was compelled to gamble until everything was lost. Suicide seemed the only alternative available to him.

Mike Brubaker's instincts had been right when he saw Alex that September morning. Alex had hit bottom and seemed to be willing to do whatever it would take to stop gambling.

No Little Plans

As he was driving north to San Francisco, Mike had made plans for an intervention with Alex. First, he would talk privately with Alex's mother and brother to enlist their support in convincing Alex to seek help. Second, the three of them as a group would confront Alex about his gambling and encourage him to seek treatment. Such a confrontation is known in the addictions treatment field as an intervention and can be a very effective technique. Confronted by family and friends, addicts are usually unable to defend themselves and will frequently submit to treatment.

Mike also planned to speak with Anna Petros about her practice of loaning Alex money to cover his gambling losses. He wanted her to tell Alex point blank that if he refused to seek help, she would no longer bail him out.

As for treatment, Mike would offer Alex two options. He

could seek treatment for compulsive gambling at a psychiatric hospital on the East Coast or he could enter the Community Hospital Recovery Center program in Monterey for simultaneous treatment of his alcohol, drug, and gambling problems.

Upon seeing Alex at his mother's home, Mike realized a formal intervention probably wouldn't be necessary. He decided to forego the private meeting with Anna Petros and Tony and to go straight to the problem of laying out the options to Alex in the presence of his mother and brother. Alex looked ready and indeed he was. He agreed he needed help and opted for the Monterey treatment program. Mike, who was surprised at how smoothly the process had gone, would say later, "For years, the family had treated Alex's gambling as a deep, dark family secret. It was quite a step for Mrs. Petros to call me in the first place, much less go along with a plan of treatment for Alex."

Despite Alex's compliance, Mike sensed that he was anxious and somewhat leery about entering treatment. He suspected Alex might try to bolt. But the following day, after consulting with his psychologist and his girlfriend, Julie, Alex showed up at the recovery center accompanied by his mother to begin a four-week treatment program.

As supervisor of the center's adult treatment program, Brubaker met with the treatment staff on Monday and helped map out a course of treatment for Alex. Brubaker assigned a straight-talking, no-nonsense counselor to Alex, whose treatment would consist of full participation in the program's alcoholism and drug dependency treatment program, supplemented by individual therapy sessions on gambling and compulsory attendance at the Thursday night Gamblers Anonymous meeting, which was held on the treatment center grounds. Mike's contact with Alex was minimal during treatment, but he did see his patient at a group therapy session later in the first week of treatment. Mike felt a sense of deep personal satisfaction when he heard a relaxed, cheerful Alex Petros introduce himself to the group as a recovering addict and compulsive gambler. Alex Petros had begun the long process of recovery from compulsive gambling.

On a beautiful Sunday morning about a month after he had completed treatment at the Community Hospital Recovery Center, Alex Petros sat with Mike Brubaker at the kitchen table in Alex's two-story Carmel home. The two would be joining Len Baltzer, administrator of the Community Hospital Recovery Center, around noon for a round of golf at one of the demanding courses on the Monterey Peninsula. Alex also was trying to tempt Mike to join him and his friend Gus for another round of golf on Tuesday at Spyglass Hill, one of the three courses used in the Bing Crosby Pro-Am Golf Tournament.

LAUGHING AT ADVERSITY— AND HIMSELF

Early recovery was kind to Alex, and over coffee, pastries, and cigarettes, Alex reminisced about his gambling and recovery. Within a month, he was entertaining the very people who had helped rescue him. He talked freely about his gambling, struggling only when he tried to describe the numbing depression he experienced after losing. Alex was now spending much of his time in Carmel and was a regular at the Gamblers Anonymous (GA) meetings in nearby Monterey. He also was seeing his psychologist two times a week and said he believed he was making progress.

Peculiar to Alex, one of his biggest concerns was having too much idle time. A wealthy bachelor, he threw himself into golf with a passion. When that was not enough to fill his days, he took up gardening. He was planning to devote a whole day to planting bulbs in the garden surrounding his $750,000 home when his girlfriend, Julie, called to tell

him that her Porsche had been damaged in an auto accident. Alex had given the car to her as a present and even
though he sympathized with Julie about the accident, he
noticed for the first time that he could laugh about such a
thing. Julie had been upset, but Alex had been able to view
with humor her recounting of the accident. Now, reminisc-
ing with Mike Brubaker, Alex could not only laugh at adver-
sity, but at himself as well.

He recalled his first try at Gamblers Anonymous. About
a year earlier, he had attended a meeting in San Francisco
at the recommendation of his psychologist and had been
turned off immediately by the down-and-out look of the
group. "There were two guys there straight from the
Golden Gate Bridge," he said. "The police had talked them
out of jumping off the bridge." The San Francisco meeting
unnerved him, but a few months later he began attending a
meeting in Monterey that was vastly different. He felt comfortable in a group that appeared more genteel and closer
to his self-image and lined up a sponsor to help him over
the rough spots. He also had an Alcoholics Anonymous
sponsor and was attending AA meetings in Monterey on a
regular basis. Unlike many compulsive gamblers, Alex had
the resources to solve whatever financial problems he had.
He owed $270,000 to his mother, but planned to "sell off
something" to repay her. "My mother is not insisting on the
money," he said, "but I need to pay her back as part of my
recovery program. The money I borrowed from her was to
cover my gambling losses."

Alex credited Betty, his treatment counselor at the Community Hospital Recovery Center, with turning him
around. He said he was a "whipped puppy" when he entered the hospital, but that he was fairly upbeat now. "Betty
taught me that I had to quit gambling and using [drugs]
for myself—not for my family," he said. "I have to lick it for
me and for me alone. Even your family can sabotage your
recovery. When I checked into the center, I fully expected
my family's support while I was there. But when we got

down to the nitty-gritty of treatment, my mother and brother backed out on me. Only Julie stuck with me. I think my family was afraid that I would embarrass them if they showed up for family therapy. At first, I felt all alone, but Betty helped me through that. In fact, if anything, when my family backed out on me, it proved to me I was there for myself. I had thought about walking out, but I didn't. I stayed for me."

FINDING A PURPOSE

Alex was exploring business opportunities to give structure and purpose to his life. One business he wasn't considering was the restaurant business, where, he said, drugs were commonplace. He didn't want to expose himself to the temptation of drugs and alcohol. "I want to do something that is healthy for me," he said. Alex was also planning a trip to England with Julie in November and was thinking about buying a house outside London. Mike Brubaker was not in favor of the trip. He thought Alex needed to stay close to home and his support system during the early months of recovery. Though Alex listened to Mike, he wasn't swayed. He said he would locate a list of GA meetings in England before he left and would attend some meetings while he was there. Alex said he believed his gambling days were behind him, but he knew it wouldn't be an easy process. "I've got to keep plugging along a little at a time," he said, "and I've never done that before. I have to change my whole life-style. That's not going to be easy, but I've got to do it." Somehow, in his mind Alex viewed the trip to London as part of the "change in my whole life-style." Although Mike would argue with him, Alex was adamant. With his abstinence from gambling and drugs intact, Alex and Julie left for an extended trip to London.

Mike Brubaker knew the trip was not a good idea, but he also knew through years of experience that Alex's recovery was out of his hands. It was up to Alex now. Like thousands of other recovering compulsive gamblers, Alex alone was responsible for mastering the deadly odds that would confront him on a daily basis for the rest of his life.

3

CARRYING THE MESSAGE

Before he left for England, Alex Petros told Mike Brubaker about his experience of winning $650,000 at a casino blackjack table. A look of amazement came over Mike's face. Finally, after an uncharacteristic silence, Mike said, "You know, $650,000 is more than twice what I earned in twenty years in the Navy."

Mike, a retired Navy veteran with a quick mind for numbers, seemed temporarily transfixed by the comparison, but then shrugged it off. Fantasizing about great sums of money is a luxury Mike can no longer afford. Once he had entertained dreams of winning $100,000 at the blackjack tables in Las Vegas and gaining financial independence for the first time in his life. He had envisioned using his winnings to pay off his car and his mortgage and to set aside a little for his son and daughter's education. He never came close to winning $100,000, but the dream persisted throughout his gambling days. Mike now knows that his thoughts of putting his winnings to good use were delusional. If he had won $100,000 or even a fraction of that amount, he would have set aside the biggest chunk of it as his gambling stash and tried to parlay that into more money. "I could never get enough money," he would say. He knew that, like Alex, he would have lost the whole bundle sooner or later, along with all the things that he had intended to pay off with the money. But, unlike wealthy Alex, Mike would not have had anything left to fall back on.

A Personal Twelve-Step Recovery

Eleven years after making his last bet on a golf course, Mike has no illusions about gambling or his ability to control his gambling once he begins. After a life of betting on everything from balls and strikes at a baseball game to horse-races, Mike considers himself a nongambler in a world awash with gambling activities. Even after eleven years of not gambling, Mike still takes extraordinary pains to avoid the slightest temptation to gamble. He has stricken Las Vegas and the other gambling spots of Nevada from his travel itinerary, and he studiously avoids lotteries, raffles, auctions, office pools, card games, magazine sweepstakes, scratch-off cards for free food and drinks at restaurants, racetracks, the stock market, and speculative investments. In addition, he refrains from watching game shows on television and shuns all forms of gambling lingo such as *bet* or *wager.*

Even more importantly, Mike has immersed himself in a personal Twelve-Step self-help program of recovery from compulsive gambling. He also has embarked on an active crusade to spread the word about the problem of compulsive gambling and to help other compulsive gamblers such as Alex Petros quit gambling. Mike is well-suited for the task. He is an energetic, loquacious, and wildly enthusiastic fifty-one-year-old who believes fervently in the redemptive powers of recovery and his ability to reach people and affect change in their lives.

He comes by his beliefs naturally. He has made dramatic

changes in his own life—first, when he overcame his long struggle with alcoholism in 1974, after repeated failures to stop drinking, and again in 1978, when he conquered his destructive gambling addiction. He has no doubt whatsoever that by surrendering to his addiction and entering recovery he saved his life. Following his recovery from alcoholism he earned certification as an alcoholism counselor in the U.S. Navy's renowned Alcoholism Rehabilitation Service and helped hundreds of people, including many famous ones, overcome their problems with alcoholism.

He wants desperately to have a similar impact on compulsive gambling and has no doubt that in time he can pull it off. He knows, however, that it won't be easy. Few people are willing to acknowledge the seriousness of the problem of compulsive gambling and far too many compulsive gamblers are unwilling to seek help for their problem. Mike hopes to change that. He confronts alcohol and drug patients he suspects of being compulsive gamblers and encourages them to get help. "Gambling is a big relapse issue for drug and alcohol patients," Mike says. "One big win or loss and they get loaded."

In the fall of 1989, Brubaker, an imposing figure at 6 feet, 2 inches, and 200 pounds, coerced an alcohol/drug patient at the Community Hospital Recovery Center into attending the Thursday night Gamblers Anonymous meeting on the hospital grounds. The patient, Vinnie Maggio, an outgoing thirty-four-year-old Italian restaurant manager, was wearing a T-shirt from a racetrack the first time he met Mike. Vinnie said Mike gave him the once-over and inquired, "Is there another problem you ought to be looking at while you're here, Vinnie?" That's all Brubaker said to Vinnie about his gambling, but it was enough. Vinnie recounts, "From that point on, it seemed like every time I was talking about gambling, Mike would appear. It was uncanny. I tried to avoid him, but one time when I was sneaking around in the hallway waiting for a chance to call my bookie, I rounded a corner and ran smack-dab into Mike. He just looked me square in the eye and said, 'How are you doing, Vinnie?' He intimidated the hell out of me. Finally, I decided to go to the meeting just to get Mike off my back. I ended up listening to what the people were saying. I discovered pretty quickly that I might be a compulsive gambler as well as an alcoholic. This was my second treatment for alcoholism. I had been sober for two years before I drank again. While I was sober, I had more money and my gambling escalated. I was losing my whole paycheck some weeks. Eventually I resumed drinking. I lost my job because of my drinking, but still I kept betting on baseball and football."

PLANTING THE SEED

Brubaker laughs about the episode with Vinnie. He says, "All I do is ask a question to plant a seed about gambling. If you are a compulsive gambler, that's all it takes. The paranoia takes over, like it did with Vinnie." Mike is equally confrontational when he's proselytizing about the problem of compulsive gambling. Recently he was staffing an exhibit booth at a large national conference for alcoholism counselors in San Francisco when an unsuspecting convention coordinator dropped by to see if he was satisfied with the arrangements for exhibitors. The bewildered woman received more input than she had bargained for. Mike launched into a three-minute dissertation about the profusion of raffles and auctions in the exhibit area and about the practice of giving away door prizes to registrants. He told her that addictions counselors should be more sensitive to the fact that millions of people are addicted to gambling. "It's like having an open bar on the exhibit floor," he said. "It gives out the wrong message." When the coordinator left, Mike shrugged. "Maybe it did some good," he said.

"Maybe next year she'll at least raise the question about raffles and door prizes."

Mike also is not averse to haranguing fast-food restaurant managers about handing out scratch-off cards for hamburgers, soft drinks, and the like to children. "It introduces them to gambling at an early age," he says. He will call up newspaper and television reporters to complain about errors in a story on gambling or to alert them to certain truths about the nature of compulsive gambling.

The day the scandal broke about major league baseball's investigation into Pete Rose's gambling activities, Mike got on the phone to a television reporter he knew in Monterey and urged him not to overlook compulsion as an angle to the story. Although the Monterey reporter didn't bite on his tip, Mike felt a sense of vindication later when the national media began focusing on Pete Rose's gambling habits. "The Rose publicity helped our cause immensely," Mike says. "Probably more has been written in the press about compulsive gambling since the Pete Rose case surfaced than was written in the previous five or ten years."

Brubaker still believes, however, that the true message about compulsive gambling hasn't gotten through clearly in the Rose affair. He says the legal issue of whether Rose bet on baseball has obscured the fact that compulsive gambling may have been the underlying cause of Rose's actions. He says many people still don't see anything wrong with an athlete's excessive gambling as long as he avoids betting on his sport and specifically on his own team. Brubaker says the real issue relates to sickness, "If Rose is a compulsive gambler, he is a sick man and can't control his gambling. If that's so, he was bound to bet on baseball sooner or later regardless of the rules prohibiting it. Baseball's the sport he knows best and gamblers are always looking for an edge to try to recoup their losses. He wouldn't have given the fact that he was risking suspension a second thought. He would have thought, 'What the hell—they'll never find out.' That's the way we compulsive gamblers think. Taking risks is part of the action. We don't believe we are ever going to lose or get caught doing something we shouldn't. A baseball player who gets caught breaking the rules is not very different than an accountant who gets caught embezzling funds to pay off his gambling debts. The only difference is the accountant usually winds up in jail."

THE LOTTERY TRAP

Brubaker believes more people are becoming aware of compulsive gambling. And because it is a serious sickness, he believes it's none too soon. Mike is concerned that gambling is rapidly becoming part of the fabric of American life with the proliferation of state lotteries, some of which have been expanded in some states to include professional sports betting. Especially upset about the methods used to promote the lotteries, Mike has put together a collection of ads, assorted newspaper clippings, and bric-a-brac that he uses to illustrate the lengths to which the state of California goes to entice people to play the lottery.

One of the clippings from the *Los Angeles Times* describes the advertising contract for the California State Lottery as the choicest plum in the California advertising market, worth about $60 million a year. Mike bristles at the use of celebrities such as Olympic star Greg Louganis in lottery ads and the basic advertising theme depicting ordinary people dreaming of buying yachts, luxury cars, and mansions with their lottery winnings. "Let's take a close look at what's going on," Mike says. "The state government is now in the business of promoting gambling to its citizens. You would think that the lottery people would at least have the decency to point out that gambling can be addictive and make some funds available for education and treatment. The ironic part about it all is that a lot of poor people are using their state welfare checks to buy state lottery tickets. And who can blame them? They are the people to whom the advertising is most likely to appeal."

Mike is opposed to lotteries in general, but he's not antigambling. He believes the great majority of people can—and do—gamble for fun and recreation. He is quick to point out, however, that gambling is not entertainment. "Gambling is gambling, period," he says. He believes there are millions of people like himself who are addicted to gambling, and that many of them are easy prey for powerful advertising messages designed to lure them to buy lottery tickets at the corner grocery store. Worse yet, he believes, the lottery, as well as other forms of easily accessible, legal gambling activities, introduces thousands of would-be compulsive gamblers to gambling. "There are a lot of people buying lottery tickets today who wouldn't dream of going to a racetrack or a casino, much less engaging in some illegal gambling activity," Brubaker says. "And some of them are going to get hooked and end up spending their grocery money on lottery tickets. That person may be your mother, your grandmother, your son, or your daughter. There's no way of predicting who it will be."

Brubaker uses his lottery paraphernalia as props for the lectures he gives on compulsive gambling to a variety of audiences. Through his ties with the alcohol- and drug-treatment field, Mike is in demand as a speaker on gambling at alcoholism treatment centers and at workshops and conferences on addictive behavior. He also speaks to service clubs, professional organizations, and students at high schools and colleges. As he scoots around on the lecture tour by car or plane on days off from work, Mike resembles an old-fashioned traveling salesman. He has with him his briefcase full of lottery items, a second- or third-generation copy of a videotape of his presentation, a few dog-eared overhead slides, and reams of notes on gambling, which he constantly updates for his speeches.

• • •

HITTING THE ROAD

In the tradition of circuit speakers in Alcoholics Anonymous and Gamblers Anonymous, Mike rarely charges a fee for his appearances. Usually, only his expenses are covered. When he does collect a fee, he invariably invests it in a new videotape or a book to supplement his presentation. Not a man of means, he has not taken a vow of poverty. Someday he would like very much to be able to support himself on the lecture circuit and to have the time and money to travel from coast to coast talking to groups and individuals about compulsive gambling and recovery.

Knowledgeable and dedicated experts on pathological gambling—such as Dr. Richard J. Rosenthal, Dr. Henry R. Lesieur, Dr. Durand F. (Dewey) Jacobs, Dr. Julian Taber, Dr. Robert Politzer, Dr. Valerie Lorenz, and the late Dr. Robert L. Custer—have made great strides in the diagnosis and treatment of compulsive (or pathological) gambling disorders, in the dissemination of information, and in both the collection and the publication of research on the disease. But Mike knows from experience that the best way to carry the message to the mass of compulsive gamblers is for compulsive gamblers to hit the road much like Bill Wilson, Dr. Bob Smith, and the legions of other recovering alcoholics did in the formative years of Alcoholics Anonymous.

Mike loves to speak on the subject of compulsive gambling. He claims that it gives him a high similar to the one he experienced with gambling. An impassioned speaker given to a staccato delivery, he paces back and forth in front of an audience with a portable microphone in one hand and a pointer in the other. Mike talks about gambling and compulsive gambling in general as well as his own problem with gambling and his long road to recovery. His remarks are extemporaneous, so no two of his lectures are alike. As a result, he constantly adjusts the videotape aspect of his presentation to get it into sync with what he actually says.

Mike peppers his remarks with humorous or bizarre anecdotes and shocking statistics. After an hour, he opens up his presentation for a question-and-answer-period with no time limit. Having invited members of the audience to join him after the lecture to discuss anything that's on their minds, he will eventually adjourn to a coffee shop for a long rap session. Invariably, the participants are compulsive gamblers or the spouses of compulsive gamblers. In November 1978, Mike was one of the people from an audience who tagged along with a speaker for coffee after a presentation on gambling at the Naval Hospital in Long Beach. His life hasn't been the same since.

4

ONE LAST FLING

Mike Brubaker's life today is in sharp contrast to what it was in the 1960s and 1970s, when he would escape from the tedium of everyday life to chase his dream of riches at the blackjack tables in Las Vegas or at the racetracks around Los Angeles. In the 1980s Mike was supervisor of the adult inpatient and outpatient alcoholism and drug dependency treatment programs at the Community Hospital Recovery Center, a graceful sixty-three-year-old Spanish-style structure with manicured grounds and a massive iron entry door opening into a tasteful interior. He worked out of a cozy first-floor office decorated with autographed pictures of Senator Herman Talmadge of Georgia, former First Lady Betty Ford, and Billy Carter, all of whom were patients under Mike's care in the late 1970s at Long Beach Naval Hospital. Among these photos is one of Mike shaking hands with President Jimmy Carter in the White House. The bookcase above Mike's desk is crammed full of books on alcoholism and gambling and mementos of Mike's recovery from alcoholism. Included among the memorabilia is Mike's extensive collection of statues and other replicas of camels. Mike adopted the camel as a symbol of recovery from alcoholism because of the animal's remarkable ability to survive for long periods of time without drinking.

A M E N T O R ' S   H E L P

At the Recovery Center in Monterey, Mike was reunited with Len Baltzer, the administrator of the facility and a highly respected figure in California chemical dependency treatment circles. Baltzer, a retired U.S. Navy chief with more than twenty-two years of recovery from alcoholism, was responsible for luring Brubaker to Monterey from Los Angeles in 1988. The two men met in 1974 in Long Beach. Baltzer was a counselor at Long Beach while Mike was undergoing treatment there for alcoholism. Later Baltzer assumed the role of mentor to Mike as Brubaker pursued his own career in the alcoholism treatment field, first at the Naval Hospital and then at a number of private hospitals and clinics following his retirement from the Navy.

Colleagues who worked with the two men in the Navy Alcohol Rehabilitation Service generally credit Baltzer, a well-organized, immaculate, taciturn man, with being a stabilizing influence in Mike's life. They now have a comfortable working relationship and have frequently played golf together at the lush seaside courses of the Monterey Peninsula. Their closeness is evidenced by the fact that although the Recovery Center has no formal treatment program for compulsive gambling, Baltzer has given Mike the freedom he needs to reach out to compulsive gamblers in Monterey and beyond.

Len Baltzer couldn't have possibly imagined what lay ahead for him in April of 1978 when he suggested to Mike that the two of them take a short golfing vacation together. An avid low-handicap golfer, Len knew Mike shared his passion for golf and was always ready to play at a moment's notice. Mike and Len also liked to slip away on weekends whenever they could to play in tournaments all over California. Mike had quickly agreed to the idea and suggested an itinerary that would take them from their home base of Long Beach to Las Vegas and on up through the Sierra Nevada Mountains to Pebble Beach. Len okayed the plan even though he was only lukewarm to the idea of starting the trip in Las Vegas. He much preferred other courses to the long, flat Las Vegas layouts, but thought a night on the Las Vegas Strip would be a nice diversion.

What Len didn't realize was that the stop in Las Vegas was Mike's real purpose for taking the trip. Mike hoped to score big at the blackjack tables in Las Vegas in an effort to dig himself out from under a mound of personal debt. The golfing part of the trip was only incidental to Mike; it simply afforded him a good excuse to offer to his then wife, Marjorie. If he were going to be golfing the entire time, it was reasonable to leave her and their two children at home. It never occurred to Mike that he was taking advantage of Baltzer's friendship. He reasoned that Len welcomed any opportunity to play golf, and he pledged that he wouldn't let his gambling interfere with the rest of the trip. Baltzer, on his part, had no reason to suspect that Mike was a compulsive gambler. Mike had been sober for three and a half years and was making great progress as an alcoholism counselor at Long Beach Naval Hospital. In fact, the hospital had recently achieved national prominence by treating Mrs. Betty Ford, and Mike had played a key role in her treatment. Len wouldn't discover the depth of Mike's problem with gambling until several months later, when Brubaker shared his gambling story with him and apologized for his behavior on their golfing trip.

• • •

A DIFFERENT KIND OF BENDER

The golfing trip had taken a bizarre turn at the very start. Len noticed that Mike became fidgety and hyper as they approached Las Vegas near the end of their 270-mile drive from Los Angeles, and he was somewhat surprised with how quickly Mike hustled off to the casino upon their arrival. Len didn't pay much heed to his observations, however; he dismissed Mike's behavior as typical of his restless nature and set a time with Mike for the two of them to meet later that evening for dinner and a show. Baltzer planned to retire reasonably early because they had a seven o'clock tee time the following morning.

Len ended up going to dinner and the show alone. He also drove alone to the golf course the next morning after failing to find Mike in his room. Though miffed that Mike had not made contact with him, Baltzer didn't let it faze him. After a long career in the Navy and as an alcoholism counselor, very little fazed Len. He had long ago stopped babysitting adults.

Brubaker finally surfaced at the golf course about half an hour before the seven o'clock tee time. Roaring up to the clubhouse in a cab, Mike jumped out rumpled and unshaven. He dashed directly to the practice tee, where he knew he could find Len going through his regular warm-up routine. After spotting Len, Mike rushed over, offered a quick apology for being late, and asked Len if he could borrow a hundred dollars to pay for the taxi and his greens fee. Baltzer complied and then watched with amusement as Brubaker bolted off to pay the cab driver, collected his golf equipment from the cab, and scrambled to the first tee.

"I knew Mike hadn't been drinking," Baltzer recalls, "but he looked like he had been out on a bender. He was wearing the same clothes he had worn the day before; his eyes were bloodshot; and he looked real scraggly. He told me he had had a bad night at the tables and had spent the whole night trying to recoup his losses. That was all true, of course, so it was easy for me to accept it as the truth. He never once mentioned how much he had lost or indicated to me that gambling was a problem for him. I let the matter drop. I figured if Mike had something else to tell me, he would."

The rest of the golfing trip wasn't much better. Mike was forced to make a detour to Alameda in the San Francisco Bay Area to draw on a line of credit he had with the Navy Credit Union to repay Baltzer and finance what was left of the trip. Len, in fact, was barely able to salvage a round of golf at Pebble Beach before he had to catch a plane in Monterey to keep an important appointment at home. Len left his car with Mike, who drove back home alone.

Normally an energetic person, Mike was tired and despondent as he drove the 350 miles back to Long Beach. He was $1,500 deeper in debt, he had lied to his family and his closest friend, and he was beginning to feel he was losing his grip on sobriety, which was the most important thing in the world to him. Mike knew he was doomed if he started drinking again. Still, he wasn't quite ready to accept the fact that he was as hopelessly addicted to gambling as he was to alcohol. He believed he might be able to stop gambling—or at least control it—if only he could get out of debt. The only concession he was willing to make at this point was that he knew he couldn't afford to try his luck again at Las Vegas. He reasoned that he should stick to betting the ponies at Los Alamitos and try to edge himself out of debt little by little. Mike's Navy salary as a petty officer, first class, was about $15,000 a year, and his personal debts, most of which were the result of gambling, were about $30,000.

Mike Brubaker had been revved up about his trip to Las Vegas with Len Baltzer. He enjoyed playing the horses at the local tracks in the Los Angeles area and fancied himself a good handicapper. But his first love was Las Vegas. That was where the action was, and Mike had thrived on action since he was a small boy growing up in Tacoma, Washington. Even as a kid, Mike had been a fierce competitor in everything he did, and competition is what gambling is all about. From sandlot sports to parlor games with his brothers and grandparents, Mike was a competitor.

In the huge hotel casinos lining the Las Vegas Strip, Mike could play blackjack around the clock and was convinced he would strike it rich someday. Mike marveled at the action and the free flow of cash in the casinos, where crisp hundred-dollar bills were as common as quarters in a laundromat. To prepare for the trip, Mike had begun squirreling away a few hundred dollars from his paycheck (which he always cashed to prevent Marjorie from knowing the exact amount of his take-home pay) and from his and Marjorie's joint checking account. Mike suspected that Marjorie was aware of the fact that he gambled too much even though she had never confronted him about it. He believed—correctly so—that Marjorie was willing to overlook his gambling because she was so grateful that he had finally stopped drinking.

SWINGING THE ODDS

Immediately prior to his departure, Mike fattened his gambling stash by taking out a $500 loan from the Navy Credit Union in Long Beach. With more than $1,000 in hand, he figured he was all set. Previously he had parlayed a similar stake into $5,000 in a nonstop weekend of action on the Strip, and each subsequent time he headed for Nevada, Mike assumed he could do as well or better—much better, in fact. Mike considered himself to be an above-average card player and clung firmly to the belief that his skills would eventually swing the odds in his favor. He rarely, if ever, reflected on the times he had left Las Vegas for the 270-mile trek home without enough money for gas or food.

He figured losses were just part of the game. To be on the safe side, however, Mike usually filled up his car with gas upon arriving in Las Vegas.

By the time he and Len Baltzer arrived in Las Vegas in the afternoon, Mike was so pumped up that the palms of his hands were moist, his heart was beating rapidly, and he was talking even faster than usual. He managed to keep a lid on his excitement when Baltzer accompanied him to the casino at the hotel where they were staying. He didn't want Baltzer to observe him in a gambling frenzy; he was afraid Len might think he had a gambling problem. Just as Mike expected, Baltzer tired quickly of the casino activity and announced he was retiring to his room to rest and watch a little television before dinner. As soon as Len disappeared in the elevator, Mike vanished from the hotel in a flash. His destination was the Circus Circus Casino on the Strip, where circus acrobats performed high-wire acts above the casino floor and patrons from the three-thousand-room hotel were packed elbow to elbow at the slots and gaming tables in the expansive windowless casino.

Circus Circus was Mike's favorite casino because they dealt blackjack from single decks of cards. Most of the other casinos had begun using three or four decks at a time to speed up the action, but Mike preferred the single deck because he felt he could keep better track of the cards. He spent the next twelve hours at Circus Circus and at the nearby Stardust Hotel Casino, where they also dealt single-deck blackjack. He felt no pangs of guilt about standing up Baltzer for dinner. The first time he seriously considered joining his best friend was at six o'clock the following morning when the dealer raked away his last five-dollar chip from the table. If he had won that bet or a few others along the way, Mike would have left Baltzer to play golf alone. In fact, Mike's favorite time to gamble was in the early morning hours, when only the serious gamblers remained at the tables.

• • •

S U S T A I N I N G T H E P L E A S U R E

As it was, the $1,000-plus stake Mike had amassed for the Las Vegas fling was completely gone and he had nowhere else to go except the golf course. He felt guilty about losing the money and abandoning Baltzer, but he was determined to put on a happy face and naively hoped to salvage the remainder of the trip. Mike had lost his stash little by little in five- and ten-dollar increments. Like Alex Petros, Mike followed a progressive betting pattern, although for much smaller stakes. He would open up by betting five to ten dollars per hand and would double his bet to ten or twenty dollars each time he won. Each time he lost, he would back off and return to the five-to-ten-dollar level until he won again. Mike seldom threw caution to the wind. He hardly ever varied from his betting pattern. For one thing, the strategy enabled him to stay in the game longer. If he were to double up to chase his losses as some high rollers do, he would run the risk of tapping out in the early going. That thought bothered him more than losing. What he craved most from gambling was the action. He would go to any lengths to stay in the game, even if it meant minimizing his chances of a big score by sticking to a relatively conservative betting scheme. At times, Mike had even loaned money to other players just to keep the action going. In a way, it was like trying to drink slowly: the slower an alcoholic drinks, the longer the duration, the longer the pleasure.

Mike was not a flamboyant gambler in the style of Alex Petros. Instead, he camped out at either end of the blackjack table (he refers to the spots as "first base" and "third base") and, blending in with the crowd, he played for hours on end with a stoic expression on his face. At any given time in Las Vegas, hundreds of gamblers like Mike sit astride the stools at the blackjack tables or stare impassively at the video poker screens as they rapidly manipulate the buttons to operate the machines.

Eleven years later, Mike would observe, "We are the typical compulsive gamblers, not the Alexes or the Pete Roses of the world. We are average people with average jobs who gamble from paycheck to paycheck. Most of us can't afford to lose a few hundred dollars, much less a thousand. Gambling isn't fun to us; it's an escape, an obsession. You become numb."

Although he didn't realize it fully at the time, the trip to Las Vegas actually signaled the beginning of the end of Mike Brubaker's days as a compulsive gambler.

RIGOROUS HONESTY

Fortunately for Mike, he had been exposed to a program of recovery from alcoholism that "demands rigorous honesty." The book *Alcoholics Anonymous*, which serves as the bible of recovery for many alcoholics, clearly states, "Rarely have we seen a person fail who has thoroughly followed our path. Those who do not recover are . . . usually men and women who are constitutionally incapable of being honest with themselves. . . . They are naturally incapable of grasping and developing a manner of living which demands rigorous honesty."

Those words began to haunt Mike, particularly when he was counseling alcoholic patients or taking part in self-help meetings in Los Alamitos across the street from the racetrack near Long Beach. Although he considered himself dedicated to his self-help meeting, he was finding that he was more consumed with rushing across the street after the meeting to lay down a bet than he was in what was being said at the meeting. The feelings of guilt always vanished while he was at the track, but they returned the minute the last race was run. And he was beginning to find that the feelings persisted even when he won. He was depressed and was having difficulty sleeping at night. Mike was beginning to realize that he hadn't truly achieved a state of recovery from his alcoholism. He had merely substituted one addiction for another.

Mike continued to gamble sporadically at the racetrack in sums of $100 and $200 for several months after returning to Long Beach from Las Vegas, but in November, he decided to take a tentative first step to address his gambling. The Long Beach Naval Hospital regularly invited addiction treatment experts and recovering alcoholics to speak to alcoholic patients and their families as a part of its patient education program. At a staff meeting, Mike suggested that the hospital invite someone to speak to the group about compulsive gambling. The staff concurred and in November 1978, two compulsive gamblers, a businessman named Al who had lost millions gambling and another man named Dick, came to the hospital on a Tuesday morning to talk about gambling.

ONE LAST WAGER

Mike doesn't recall how the patients responded to the talk, but he hung on to every word. Afterward, Mike asked Al and Dick to join him for lunch in the hospital cafeteria. He didn't admit to the two men that he had a problem with gambling, but he realized that they probably had guessed as much from the questions he asked them. Mike identified with everything Al and Dick said. Both men strongly recommended Gamblers Anonymous for anyone with a problem. Eventually Mike asked Al, "What's the biggest bet you ever made?"

"Fifty thousand dollars," Al replied.

"Did you win or lose?"

"I lost," Al said.

"What would you have done if you had won?"

"I'd have bet the whole bundle, a hundred thousand dollars, on the next hand," Al replied without hesitating.

Mike could have predicted Al's final response. Mike knew he would have done the same thing. He finally realized that he too couldn't control his gambling and that the only solution available to him was to quit gambling altogether. Mike decided to attend a self-help meeting the following night at the Crystal Cathedral in nearby Garden Grove. But first, he had a golf date with Len Baltzer, with whom he had a standing wager. Mike won the bet and told Len that it was the last wager he would ever make; he was going to a self-help meeting that night. Len paid up and gave his pal a firm handshake and a hug.

That night, November 25, 1978, Mike Brubaker stood up and admitted in front of a large group of his peers that he was a compulsive gambler and that he was powerless over his gambling. He experienced the same sense of relief he had four years earlier when he had admitted he was an alcoholic. After the meeting, Mike went straight home and told Marjorie he had been to a meeting and had admitted that he was a compulsive gambler. He thought Marjorie was going to faint. Finally, she said, "Mike, I thought you were gambling a lot, but I didn't want to talk to you about it because I was afraid you'd start drinking again." Mike went to another meeting the following day and the day after that and hasn't gambled since. Ironically, the two gamblers who were so helpful to Mike both resumed gambling. Al began gambling again after abstaining for a period of ten years and Dick has gambled off and on for the past eleven years.

5

THE SEEDS OF ADDICTION

A s Mike Brubaker puts it, he "never did not gamble." By the time he was seven or eight years old, he was an expert pinochle player and could hold his own with older kids lagging coins, shooting marbles, or playing the nickel pinball machines around his hometown of Tacoma, Washington. Even as a youngster, Mike experienced a rush from penny-ante gambling. Winning pennies, nickels, and marbles from older kids made Mike feel smarter and better than them and gave him a sense of power. He became a street-smart hustler who enjoyed the thrill of living on the edge. He was confident that if all else failed, he could survive by his wits alone. Those feelings persisted for the next three decades as Mike gambled regularly on everything from sports to casino games. Yet he didn't begin to suspect that gambling might be a problem for him until a couple of years after he quit drinking in 1974. Up to that point, his preoccupation with drinking had in fact obscured his problem with gambling.

Born in Tacoma on May 10, 1939, Mike Brubaker is the second of four sons of Gerald and Emily Jean Brubaker. A year earlier, his parents had moved to Washington from

Manhattan, Kansas. Gerald Brubaker had been drawn to Tacoma—a bustling, industrialized port city of 150,000 people on the Puget Sound south of Seattle—by the relative prosperity of the Northwest in the late 1930s. His home state of Kansas, which depended heavily on agriculture, was still recovering from the dust bowl days of the Great Depression and good jobs were scarce there.

In his early twenties, shortly after his arrival in Washington, Gerald Brubaker took over the operation of a Mobil service station in southeastern Tacoma and operated the station for more than forty years until his retirement in 1980. He was a sturdy, no-nonsense man who worked twelve hours a day, seven days a week, and rarely had much time to spend with his family. He spent what idle time he did have bowling or fishing with his brother, who had also moved to Tacoma in the mid-1930s.

PARENTAL INFLUENCES

Mike was never close to his father. He remembers his father as a stern, strict, unaffectionate man who didn't talk much and kept primarily to himself. Gerald also liked to drink. He always kept a bottle at home and a bottle in his locker at the bowling alley. Mike suspects that his father was an unhappy man. Although Gerald had a degree in journalism from Kansas State University, he never had an opportunity to capitalize on his education. Mike knew his father wanted him and his three brothers to receive their degrees and to do better than he had done. Mike also knew his father was an alcoholic. "Dad was a maintenance drinker," Mike says. "I rarely saw him drunk, unless he was off on one of his fishing trips. He drank a certain amount each and every night after work until the day he retired. He was a good provider for us while I was growing up. He never drank at work or let his drinking interfere with his work. Once he retired, though, he began drinking more and died within two years of cirrhosis and cancer."

Mike's mother, Emily Jean, was the exact opposite of her husband. She was a large, friendly woman who served as the neighborhood mom to all the children up and down McKinley Avenue. Mike knew he could always count on his mother for affection and support and he would turn to her after disagreements with his father. "My mother held things together for us," Mike says. "She was a nurturing person—full of hugs and love. She was easily the most popular person in our neighborhood." Unfortunately, Emily Jean Brubaker's health was fragile. After ten years of trying to control her high blood pressure with medication, she died suddenly in 1960 from a stroke at the age of forty-three.

Mike was devastated by his mother's death. He was a twenty-year-old Navy seaman stationed in Japan when he received news of Emily Jean's death. He got rip-roaring drunk on the train from his base to Tokyo and stayed that way on the long trip back home to Tacoma. He winces at the memory of how empty the big house on McKinley Avenue felt when he arrived home the day after his mother's funeral. He felt all alone in the world. The only people at home to comfort him were his grandparents from Kansas. As usual, his father was working at the service station.

EARLY ADDICTION

With his mother gone, Mike felt alienated at home. He had never been particularly close to his brothers and he felt that his father didn't approve of him. He regarded himself as the black sheep of the family. Mike was bright, but school bored him and he dropped out of high school before his senior year to join the Navy. His father was openly disappointed with his performance in school. Mike's younger brothers, David and Russell, graduated from college and his older brother, Mills, attended college. "My father was never verbally abusive to me," Mike says. "He said he just couldn't understand why someone so bright couldn't do any better in school. He was a highly opinionated man and was unwilling to look at anything from someone else's point of view."

Mike had tried to earn his father's approval in other ways. Before he joined the Navy, he had worked hard at his job of washing cars and pumping gas at his father's service station and he excelled at sports. He also tagged along with his father on his regular visits to the bowling alley and on his fishing trips. But nothing seemed to improve their relationship. His father's priority for his sons was education and Mike felt he had failed him. "I desperately wanted my father's approval," Mike says, "but I never felt like I measured up. I don't ever recall my father hugging me or telling me he loved me."

The trips to the bowling alley with his father, however, held other rewards for Mike. The bowling alley quickly became one of his favorite haunts. He reveled in the atmosphere. He liked the sound of the heavy balls on the hardwood lanes, the rattling of the pins, the camaraderie, and the loud talk of men drinking, betting, and having a good time. Mike got a job at the bowling alley setting pins and spent his wages bowling and playing the pinball machines for hours on end. The pinball machines paid off in nickels for high scores and Mike soon became one of the best pinball players in the place.

Mike's final split with his father came when he was sixteen and working at the service station. By then Mike was drinking heavily with his friends and was skipping class to hang out at the bowling alley and arcades before reporting to work. Mike says he was an alcoholic by the age of fifteen. "I would get drunk and party every weekend," he says. "I hung out with a couple of other guys and I would drink three or four beers out of every sixpack we bought. I was also the one who always seemed to get caught. I would crash a car, get caught for being underage at a liquor store, everything. Nobody else seemed to get caught. I thought I was unlucky." By the age of sixteen, Mike had also developed a strong dislike for authority, much of which was directed at his father. He resented the low wages his father paid him and constantly groused about his pay to his father, his mother, and his friends. Gerald Brubaker turned a deaf ear to his son's complaints until Mike took matters into his own hands. Needing more money to support his new life-style of drinking, shooting pool, playing arcade games, and partying on weekends, Mike began stealing a dollar or two at a time from the service station till. Mike would ring up three or four dollars on the cash register for a five-dollar purchase and pocket the difference. He justified his actions by reasoning that he was taking only what was rightfully his.

Gerald Brubaker soon began to notice the discrepancy between the amount of gas sold and the receipts and confronted Mike about it. Mike considered denying the theft, but confessed. "I never remember feeling so small, so embarrassed," he says. "My father didn't say much, but I could sense that I had lost his trust forever." Fortunately for Mike, the episode and its resulting shame had a lasting effect on him. Despite the fact that he was sorely tempted on occasion, he never again stole money—unlike so many compulsive gamblers.

Shortly after the theft incident at the station, when he turned seventeen, Mike decided to enlist in the Navy. He craved independence—or so he thought—and he laughs today about his decision to join the Navy. "I hated authority and wanted independence and wound up spending the next twenty-two years of my life in the Navy. That doesn't make a hell of a lot of sense, does it?"

Mike found a home in the U.S. Navy, although his penchant for getting into trouble dogged him throughout most of his career. Virtually all of his trouble was the result of drinking. From 1958 to 1974, when he quit drinking, he was written up by his superiors for nineteen alcohol-related offenses. Otherwise, his service record was impeccable. He even earned a top-level security clearance while stationed in San Francisco in the early 1970s as a radar man plotting the movement of U.S. ships in the Pacific.

SAFE HAVEN

Typical of his regular performance reviews in the Navy was a June 1, 1971, review in which the commanding officer rated Mike as excellent or good in the five performance categories but noted, "During this marking period, Petty Officer Brubaker has had problems with alcohol and has shown more than once a lack of awareness of his position as supervisor." In another report a year earlier, the commanding officer had observed, "Brubaker has had a recurring problem with his drinking, which on one occasion inconvenienced the command. His overall performance has outweighed the problem and proper guidance can prevent its occurrence in the future."

Mike jokes about these reports today and produces them on occasion to illustrate points in his lectures on alcoholism. Though it's less so today, the Navy was a safe haven in the 1960s and 1970s for rambunctious enlisted men like Mike, despite the specter of the Vietnam War. "I always had a place to sleep and eat," he says, "and I couldn't get fired as long as I performed my duties. The Navy was a very forgiving employer. It was the military way of life back then."

Less forgiving was Mike's first wife, Marjorie, his childhood sweetheart in Washington whom he married on April 28, 1960, while he was home on leave following his mother's death. The Brubakers' marriage lasted through some stormy times for twenty-six years before ending in divorce in 1986. "Marjorie's big mistake was marrying me in the first place," Mike says. "She knew I was an alcoholic when she married me. I think she thought marriage would reform me. I wanted to get married right away after my mother's death. I thought Marjorie could take the place of my mother in my life. I got drunk on our wedding day. I was drinking and gambling with my brother Mills and some other guys at a place in Tacoma called the Duck's Tavern. It's a wonder I didn't kill both Marjorie and myself driving to our honeymoon spot north of Tacoma. I was in a black-out and don't even remember driving. Also, I was so drunk on our wedding night that I couldn't perform sexually."

Mike says Marjorie was on him constantly about his drinking and carousing at bars. He shrugged it off, however. He thought, "What right does she have criticizing me for having a little fun?" Probably the only reason the Brubakers' marriage survived in the early years was the fact that Mike was usually at sea. Mike spent seventeen of his twenty-two years in the Navy aboard ship, which suited him fine. He had the best of two worlds: a family at home and more or less a bachelor's life at sea and in foreign ports.

FLIRTING WITH SOBRIETY

The ships were like great floating casinos to Mike, who refrained from drinking at sea if only to prove to himself that he wasn't an alcoholic. Mike spent virtually all of his off-duty hours aboard ship playing pinochle and poker, and more often than not, he reached port with a wad of cash he had won from his shipmates. "A lot of the other guys played cards for something to do on ship," he recalls. "Not me. I played to win. I wanted to put together a stash for drinking and gambling when I hit port."

Mike played the horses in Hong Kong, blackjack in Puerto Rico and Jamaica, and the slots in Europe, Japan, and other ports of call. He also drank himself into oblivion and usually reported back to ship drunk and broke. On two occasions, he missed ship altogether and was severely reprimanded. He was also reprimanded for being drunk in public (twice), sleeping in a public place in uniform, and various other minor offenses.

Mike's gambling was of little concern to the Navy since it didn't interfere with the performance of his duties. It was also of little concern to Mike at the time even though he gambled incessantly and was regularly drawing advances on his pay or borrowing from shipboard slush funds at usurious rates of interest to cover gambling debts. "Gambling was secondary to drinking," he says. "One thing I would never do was gamble away my drinking money. Drinking was too important to me." Accordingly, it was alcohol that landed Mike in big trouble. In 1965 he was dispatched to Beaumont, Texas, from the Navy Supply Depot in Seattle to serve on a precommissioning detail for a ship. He arrived in Beaumont as scheduled but got drunk and failed to report for duty. Eventually, Mike's commanding officer gathered him up and put him on an airplane for a psychiatric evaluation at the Naval Hospital in Pensacola, Florida. The psychiatrist in Pensacola diagnosed Mike as a chronic alcoholic and recommended that he attend Alcoholics Anonymous meetings.

From that point on Mike flirted with sobriety, sometimes staying dry three to six months at a time before slipping back into drinking. After the ill-fated precommissioning detail, Mike was transferred to Newport, Rhode Island, and then to Norfolk, Virginia, where in 1968 his daughter Emily was born. From Norfolk, he went to San Francisco, San Diego, and finally to Long Beach. He continued to get in trouble periodically because of his drinking, but he managed to escape serious problems until September 1974, when he got drunk in Japan and missed ship. After the Shore Patrol picked him up, Mike was placed in a Navy hospital in Japan for evaluation and was transferred back to Long Beach Naval Hospital for alcoholism treatment. He has not had a drink since.

Although he had gambled all of his life, Mike didn't have the faintest notion that gambling was a problem for him until more than two years after he had completed treatment for alcoholism in 1974. He didn't exhibit any overt signs of compulsive gambling until 1977, when he settled into a regular onshore job as an alcoholism counselor at Long Beach Naval Hospital. He gambled occasionally while being shuttled back and forth from San Francisco to San Diego, where he completed his training as an alcoholism counselor. During that period, he made a couple of trips to Reno, Nevada, and visited the tracks in Mexico and California on a few occasions. But he rarely bet more than he could afford to lose.

CRAVING ACTION

Mike thinks one reason he was able to control his gambling for more than two years is that he was focused on maintaining his sobriety and on launching a career as a counselor. "I had gotten drunk time and time again at most of the places where I gambled, so I shied away from those places in order to protect my sobriety. Once I became more secure in my sobriety and in my job, I started frequenting those places again. Also, my ego took over. I began to feel smarter and better again just like when I was a kid and began to crave action and power."

Mike also was more secure at home. Marjorie and he were getting along better than they ever had before. Their house in Long Beach had increased substantially in value since they had purchased it in 1974. Marjorie had a good job as an office manager and together they were doing well financially for the first time in their nearly twenty years of marriage. Their two children, Emily and Patrick, were also doing well. Patrick, who today is 6 feet, 6 inches tall, was a budding star basketball player and Emily was an excellent student.

If anything, things were going too well for Mike, who had grown up accustomed to action and hustling in an effort to prove himself. That motivation surfaced again when he began frequenting the Los Alamitos Racetrack. Within two years, he had brought himself and his family to the brink of disaster. Mike is convinced today that if he hadn't stopped gambling in 1978, he would have lost his sobriety, his job, his family, and his life.

6

TRADING ONE ADDICTION FOR ANOTHER

Los Alamitos Racetrack was the natural spot for Mike to begin his last big plunge into gambling. Located by the sprawling Naval and military operations complex east of Long Beach and southeast of Los Angeles, it had been like a second home to Mike Brubaker for more than fifteen years. He had become a regular at the track in the early 1960s, when he was stationed at Long Beach Naval Base. During his first tour of duty at Long Beach, he and a couple of his hard-drinking shipmates, Willie and Griff, hit Los Alamitos virtually every night when they were in port. The three of them had a system. "We detected a slight slope in the track that we thought favored the horse on the outside post," Mike recalls, "so we began betting the outside posts on short races and hit it pretty good for a while. Once we won eight or nine times in a row and thought we were pretty hot shit. We felt like we had inside information."

The three sailors were also regulars at the other tracks in the Los Angeles area. When Los Alamitos was not in session, they would head for either Hollywood Park near Los Angeles International Airport or Santa Anita, northeast of downtown Los Angeles. Usually they had the ship's disburser in tow. "We knew the disburser liked the horses, so we'd invite him along with us so we could get our pay early."

When the three shipmates weren't at the track, they hung out at Mike and Marjorie Brubaker's small house in Long Beach, drinking and playing poker well into the night or at a small bar called the Buoy Inn a block from the Brubakers' house. An enduring wife, Marjorie was tired and dismayed with her husband's life-style. "Marjorie was upset all the time," Mike says. "I'm sorry to say that I never gave her any consideration. She was working and was taking care of our son, Patrick, who was less than a year old at the time. She didn't have time to clean up after a houseful of drunks, but frankly I never gave any of that a second thought. I thought I deserved to have a little fun with my friends." The Brubakers' worst arguments, however, erupted when Marjorie would entrust Patrick to Mike's care on Saturdays while she worked. Invariably, Mike would take the toddler with him to the Buoy Inn and prop him up on a table while he drank, shot pool, and bet on the horses.

PEACE AT ALL COSTS

From the moment she first met Mike on a blind date as a teenager, Marjorie Brubaker was a key player in the long-standing drama surrounding Mike's drinking and gambling. She remembers Mike as an exciting, energetic, and handsome young man who drank too much, hung around with a rowdy group of friends, and was always skipping school. That didn't deter her, however. She figured all Mike needed was a loving farm girl from Milton, Washington, to turn him around.

Marjorie was always aware of the fact that Mike loved to gamble, but she was so focused on his alcoholism during most of their marriage that she developed a blind spot to the gambling. She considered gambling the lesser of two evils. She says Mike was secretive about his gambling. "The only time he would talk about his gambling was when he won. He would shower us with gifts or money. But I knew all along that he lost a lot, too. He was always making withdrawals of forty or sixty dollars from our account and borrowing money from the credit union or his family. I remember him borrowing sixty dollars from his dad for something and then turning around and asking his uncle for sixty dollars for the same thing. I never said a thing to him about his losses; I was trying to keep peace at all costs."

Today, Marjorie Brubaker reflects from time to time on the uncertainty of her life with Mike. She will be in a certain place or a certain city and be reminded of some of the painful events that occurred there because of Mike's drinking or gambling. "Somehow, through all the up and downs, we raised two good kids," she says, "and I'm thankful for that. Pat remembers more of what Mike did than Emily does and I believe Mike might still have a little unfinished business with Pat. But Mike's got a good relationship with both kids now."

Mike Brubaker was an inveterate horse player. He began playing the horses in his youth and played them all around the globe in his twenty-two-year career in the U.S. Navy. But from 1977 through most of 1978, he didn't merely play the horses; he was obsessed with them. At some point during that two-year period, he crossed over the fine line between heavy frequent gambling and the desperate world of compulsive gambling. Gambling had become the central focus of Mike's life. It was the last thing he thought of at night and the first thing he thought of in the morning. He pored over the racing forms at every opportunity to plot out his bets and spent literally hours each day juggling his finances to keep a steady supply of cash on hand.

• • •

JUST ONE GOOD DAY

Gone were those days of conviviality at the track with Navy pals like Willie and Griff. Mike felt he couldn't confide in anyone—even fellow gamblers. Instead, he took great pains to hide his obsession from others and lied to his friends and family about money and his whereabouts. He would lie awake at nights worrying about his finances, and he couldn't concentrate on anything other than gambling for more than a half hour or so. The only relief from his private agony was the action at the racetrack. He felt he was in control at the track and that just one good day there would magically solve the problems that were haunting him.

Mike would have preferred making regular trips to Las Vegas to feed his gambling frenzy, but he simply couldn't afford it. He felt he needed at least a $1,000 stake to make a dent at Vegas and it was becoming harder and harder for him to muster $1,000 since he was maxed out on most of his lines of credit. So he did the next best thing available to him—he played the horses. Mike could have bet at venues throughout the nation via bookies, but that didn't interest him. He liked the excitement of being at the track and laying down bets based on his own meticulous research of the racing forms. He disdained the tout sheets. He felt he was the equal of any tout and he relished the feeling of power his knowledge of the horses gave him. If he lost, he figured a fix was on.

Mike typically carried about $100 to the track and bet with precision in the early races. He always bet to win, reasoning that if a horse was good enough to place or show, it was good enough to win. Occasionally, he would lay off a place or show bet on another horse just to cover a bet, but that wasn't his usual pattern. His favorite action was the exacta, a form of betting in which one picks in exact order the first- and second-place finishers in a particular race. There was an element of sustained excitement in picking multiple winners and, of course, the payoff was substantially higher. In the early 1970s, he had scored one of his biggest wins ever ($2,500) by hitting the first exacta at Golden Gate Racetrack in San Francisco and then reeling off several winners in a row.

Despite the rush he received from gambling, Mike was not a reckless bettor. He didn't want to risk tapping out in the early going and missing out on the rest of the action. "I couldn't stand to watch a horse race without betting," he says. "Without betting, horse racing is boring, with the long waits between races." He would bet ten or twenty dollars a race in the early races and adjust his bets according to whether he was winning or losing as the session wore on. On the last race, though, he frequently bet his entire roll if he was behind. He didn't go to the track to break even; he went to win.

DASHING TO THE WINDOW

Mike also generally shied away from long shots. His favorite odds were 4 or 6 to 1, and his favorite horses were the second or third picks in a race. In 1977, when he crossed over into compulsive gambling, Mike began frequenting Los Alamitos Racetrack almost daily. He would rush from work in Long Beach, place an "early bird" bet, and then go to his regular self-help meeting for alcoholism on the military preserve across the street from the track. After the meeting, he scurried back across the street to the track, where he holed up in the first-class section of the grandstands for the remainder of the session. "I hardly heard a word that was said in the last part of our self-help meeting," he recalls. "I became really impatient if somebody talked too long. Afterward, I would feel guilty about feeling that way. Here was somebody pouring their guts out and I wasn't even listening because I was eager to get to the track. What made the guilt doubly worse is that I was an alcoholism counselor and I wasn't behaving as though I cared about recovery. But the very next night I would find myself becoming impatient again. That's how screwed up and out of control I was."

When Los Alamitos was not in session, Mike made the pilgrimage to Hollywood Park or to Santa Anita for day races whenever possible. That required cunning and speed on weekdays, since the two tracks are located almost 30 miles from Long Beach. Mike would occasionally manage to wrangle some time off during the day and drive at breakneck speed along the crowded Los Angeles freeways to reach Santa Anita or Hollywood Park in time for the first race. If Mike got mired in a traffic snarl, he would panic and begin weaving his way down service roads. "I would break out in a sweat," he recalls. "I always had my first bet planned beforehand and I knew I was going to miss a sure winner if I didn't get there in time. A lot of times I dashed to the window to lay down my first bet."

First Step Starts a New Chapter

Mike visualized winning big enough and often enough at the racetracks to bankroll excursions to Las Vegas where he could multiply his winnings. That never happened. In fact, his last trip to Vegas with Len Baltzer in April 1978 was financed primarily with borrowed money. After that failed trip, Mike turned exclusively to playing the horses as a way to alleviate his financial woes. But alleviating his financial woes proved illusory, and Mike began to fear for his sobriety. Dishonesty and guilt were overwhelming him, and these emotions outweighed whatever magic he felt at the track. He was also beginning to have thoughts of ending it all by ramming his car into a highway abutment. That's when he finally acted on his feelings by arranging for Al and Dick to speak on compulsive gambling at the Naval Hospital. The next day he went to his first self-help meeting.

During the course of that initial meeting, he felt at peace with himself for the first time in two years. He was on the path to recovery again—this time from a gambling addiction he felt was every bit as powerful as his addiction to alcohol.

Within the first few weeks of his recovery, Mike Brubaker began pondering how, with his training in counseling and his personal experience with alcoholism, he didn't recognize what was happening to him with gambling. He also began to wonder how many others like him traded one addiction for another. It was not long before he decided that he would share his message about compulsive gambling—first with other counselors and other recovering alcoholics and then with whoever would listen. A new chapter in the life of the one-time Tacoma, Washington, hustler had begun at the age of thirty-nine.

7

DEFINING
THE PROBLEM

In the days following the United States' invasion of Panama in late 1989, this small item appeared in the *Los Angeles Times*:

> LAS VEGAS—A Las Vegas oddsmaker has given 3 to 1 odds that ousted Panamanian leader Manuel A. Noriega will be caught before Christmas.
>
> Art Manteris, vice president of the Las Vegas Hilton Race and Sports Superbook, established the odds in the wake of the $1 million reward offered by the White House for Noriega's capture. Manteris noted the odds were offered for information only, since betting on non-sporting events is illegal in Nevada.

As this story illustrates, you can bet on just about anything in America. Tens of millions of people do.

Two leading national magazines reported that an estimated $208 billion was bet legally in the United States in 1988. Two hundred and eight billion dollars—that's about $800 per person for every man, woman, and child in America; more than the combined sales of the U.S. automobile industry; more than the Gross National Product of some industrialized nations.

Legalized gambling is not only big business, it's a growth industry. *Time* magazine estimates that gambling revenues have increased 57 percent in the last five years, with the hottest growth areas being lotteries (thirty-two states now have them) and slot machines.

Most of the gambling dollars—$162 billion—flow into the casinos, but there's plenty left over for state governments, federal Indian reservations, churches, card parlors, legal books, and pari-mutuels.

A New York consulting firm that surveys the gaming industry for casinos and other clients delineated the legal gambling split in 1988 as follows: casinos (table games and slot machines), $162 billion; lotteries, $17.1 billion; horse racing, $13.7 billion; bingo, $4 billion; dog racing, $3.2 billion; card rooms, $3.1 billion; other charitable games, $2.3 billion; legal bookmaking, $1.8 billion; and jai alai, $700 million.

This is only the legal take. Illegal gambling, which is still a major source of revenue for the organized crime syndicates that once controlled virtually every corner of the gambling action in the United States, is a $32-billion-a-year underground business. The lion's share of illegal betting (more than $20 billion) is placed through bookies on sporting events, which is a source of great concern to the collegiate and professional sporting establishment.

PROTECTING THE INTEGRITY OF THE GAME

As the Pete Rose gambling case demonstrated in 1989, professional sports leaders go to some length to protect what they term the integrity of their games. Beginning with the infamous 1919 World Series scandal involving the Chicago

White Sox, professional sports officials have, as a rule, dealt harshly with players, coaches, and managers who have violated the games' gambling codes, suspending such icons as Rose (major league baseball's all-time leader in base hits), Joe Jackson, Leo Durocher, Paul Hornung, and Alex Karras for gambling or associating with underworld figures.

The sports world now has a new worry—state lotteries on sporting events. Over the objections of the National Football League, the state of Oregon recently instituted a sports lottery on NFL games, and other states are considering similar moves. The public at large, however, appears to be apathetic about the increase in gambling. In fact, it appears as though everyone wants to get in on the action.

In 1989 alone, citizens in four states voted in lotteries. Municipalities such as Deadwood, South Dakota, and assorted other communities throughout the United States passed laws to permit gambling within their boundaries, and high-stake bingo games continued to proliferate on federal Indian reservations and in pockets of the Bible Belt.

In general, legalized gambling is being viewed as a panacea for raising new sources of revenue to bolster sagging economies and prop up burdened educational systems. But whatever the reason for its increased popularity, one fact seems abundantly clear: legalized gambling has entered the mainstream of everyday American life. At present, only two states—Hawaii and Utah—don't permit any form of legalized gambling within their borders.

Despite the general acceptance of legalized gambling, at least two groups other than the sports establishment and some religious organizations are casting a wary eye at the recent gambling trend in the United States. They are the National Council on Problem Gambling and a less formalized group of psychiatrists, psychologists, and researchers specializing in compulsive (or pathological) gambling, most of whom are members of the National Council. They fear that an increase in compulsive gambling problems is sure to follow any increase in legalized gambling activities.

Two concerned experts are Dr. Durand F. Jacobs, a respected California researcher and former Veterans Administration psychologist specializing in compulsive gambling, and Dr. Richard J. Rosenthal, a Los Angeles–area psychiatrist who is founder and president of the California Council on Compulsive Gambling. Both are convinced that compulsive gambling is on the rise.

CREATING A NEW GENERATION OF GAMBLERS

Jacobs estimates that the number of problem gamblers in the United States has increased by 37 percent in the last fifteen years and says that currently more than 7 million people in America have serious gambling problems. Even more ominously, Jacobs has observed a significant increase in the number of young people who gamble for money. He places the number of under-eighteen gamblers at 7 million, and says that as many as 1 million of them have experienced serious gambling-related problems.

Rosenthal is also concerned about the incidence of gambling among young people. He notes, "Today we have a population raised entirely on television. Gambling caters to our need for immediate relief and gratification, our preoccupation with material success, and a kind of action without involvement. Video games, of course, add another dimension. I've always suspected that the best research in this area was done by the casinos and gaming industry. For years now they have been devoting more and more floor space to video machines. They know how seductive video games are as a form of escape. The newer machines even pay off not in coins but in credits. You win time instead of money and, in effect, play in order to keep on playing."

Rosenthal says video gambling machines may offer gambling in its purest form. "There are fewer components and less room for the secondary rituals and fantasies associated with horse racing, for example, or poker. For the video machine player, there's an immediate stimulus-response. It is very addictive, and the trend is toward developing faster and faster games. Can you imagine what can happen when kids brought up in video arcades discover the casinos? We know almost nothing about the early TV-watching habits of compulsive gamblers, but we do know that new technologies will be bringing the video and gambling worlds closer together."

Rosenthal is concerned that the easy accessibility and heavy marketing of the new forms of legalized gambling make them more attractive for young people and he finds it ironic that the California lottery raises money for education. "At a time when there's such concern about alcohol and drug prevention programs in the schools, we are introducing a third addiction. In a few years, we will need to be adding such programs for gambling prevention."

Jacobs and Rosenthal believe that more education about gambling is necessary to reach young people and their families, but at present very little is being done in that area— even by the states that promote lotteries. Jacobs believes education and prevention efforts should begin at the primary school level and that more treatment resources should be made available to adolescent gamblers and particularly to children of adult gamblers.

Regardless of what ultimately transpires in the area of education, prevention, and treatment, experts say little can be done in the short term to stem the inevitable increase in compulsive gambling. They believe that the problem already has taken root in a new generation of gamblers and that the most that can be hoped for at the present is early treatment intervention in the progression of the problem for these gamblers.

• • •

One of the reasons compulsive gambling receives so little attention is that most people have absolutely no perception of the problem. The overwhelming majority of people who do gamble don't become compulsive gamblers. They generally set aside a certain amount of money to gamble, and quit when that money is gone. Studies done in 1988 by R. A. Volberg and H. J. Steadman indicate that while more than 80 percent of the adult population in the United States have gambled, less than 2 percent of the people are compulsive gamblers.

In addition, the compulsive gambling problem in the United States is not nearly so visible as the alcohol and drug problems in this country. Despite the white-collar crimes so frequently associated with it, compulsive gambling remains basically a silent epidemic, usually affecting only the gamblers themselves and their immediate families. Only occasionally are there headline-grabbing aspects to the problem, unlike the drunk-driving fatalities, sinister drug pushers, and South American drug cartels that so frequently make the news.

DIAGNOSING THE PROBLEM

Unfortunately, the only way many people learn about compulsive gambling is firsthand exposure to the problem. "It's surprising," Rosenthal says, "how many people with gambling problems think they are unique. They're so ashamed at not being able to control their gambling themselves. They can't believe there are others in the same boat. Many, unfortunately, are unfamiliar with GA. They just have no idea that help is available."

Compulsive gambling is a specific psychiatric disorder, which, according to the American Psychiatric Association's *Diagnostic and Statistical Manual for Mental Disorders*, third edition, revised (DSM-III-R), is characterized by "maladaptive gambling behavior." This behavior includes: frequent preoccupation with gambling or with obtaining money to gamble; frequent gambling of larger amounts of money, or gambling over a longer period of time than intended; a need to increase the size or frequency of bets to achieve the desired excitement; repeated loss of money by gambling and returning another day to win back losses; repeated efforts to reduce or stop gambling; and continuation of gambling despite an inability to pay mounting debts, or despite other significant social, occupational, or legal problems that the person knows to be exacerbated by gambling.

Rosenthal says the diagnostic criteria fall into four basic categories: progression, preoccupation, an intolerance of losing, and a disregard for consequences.

He says progression includes the notion of tolerance. The gambler cannot quit while ahead and will frequently continue to gamble until all money has been lost. Such people cannot win enough. Not only will they wager for longer periods of time and bet more than expected—they will increase the size of their bets, or the odds against them, because they require greater risks to produce a desired amount of excitement.

The second category refers to those who have a preoccupation with gambling even when they are not directly involved with it. They may be reliving past gambling experiences, handicapping or planning the next gambling venture, or thinking of ways to obtain money to gamble. Compulsive gamblers will lie to cover up the extent of involvement. Gambling is perceived as a natural response to all kinds of situations and feelings. For example, they gamble as an expression of anger, or when feeling misunderstood. Gambling is thought of as the way to solve problems, financial or otherwise, and is turned to in order to relieve boredom or restlessness.

The third category—intolerance of losing—is what leads to the act of chasing one's losses. Rosenthal says that for many gamblers, losing is not accepted as part of the game, but is taken personally. Either their self-worth is equated with the outcome of their gambling, so that they feel worthless when they lose, or they feel guilty about their gambling, and they believe they can be free of the guilt only by reversing their losses. Either way, compulsive gamblers feel the need to return to gambling as soon as possible to undo what has happened. Also, when they are losing, they will abandon their gambling strategy in an effort to rebound all at once. Losses are concealed because the gambler experiences shame about losing.

The fourth category—disregard of consequences—includes borrowing under false pretenses or beyond one's means and selling possessions, or going without necessities, to obtain money to gamble. It also includes committing or considering illegal acts such as forgery, fraud, theft, or embezzlement to finance gambling, and finally it refers to compulsive gamblers who have jeopardized or lost their marriages, families, jobs, or careers as a result of gambling.

Rosenthal is quick to add that the actual diagnosis of compulsive gambling is fairly easy to make because most compulsive gamblers don't seek help until relatively late in the course of the disorder. He adds, however, that a diagnosis is important: "It's important to be able to say why someone is a compulsive gambler, and what the essentials of the disorder are. Not only is this important for research purposes, but as the public becomes more educated about gambling, we're going to be seeing compulsive gamblers seeking help much earlier—before they get into trouble—and we're going to be seeing patients with gambling problems who are not compulsive gamblers. Treatment considerations will be very different."

Working with another psychiatrist, the late Dr. Robert Custer, and with sociologist Henry Lesieur, Rosenthal refined the diagnostic criteria of the 1992 edition of the DSM-III-R. "A large number of compulsive gamblers are being surveyed with regard to the four categories I've discussed. We want to know not only which factors best discriminate the compulsive from the noncompulsive gambler, but the best way of asking the questions to determine those factors. We'll try to determine the most essential features of the disorder, not just its similarities to alcohol and substance abuse on which the current criteria are based."

Unlike most clinicians involved in compulsive gambling, Richard Rosenthal didn't enter the field through working with alcohol and drug patients. The soft-spoken, scholarly fifty-one-year-old psychiatrist first became interested in compulsive gambling about ten years ago as a result of an enduring love affair with literature—specifically the writing of Russian novelist F. M. Dostoyevsky, an apparent compulsive gambler who wrote many of his most interesting stories and novels during the years he was most out of control. Rosenthal, who majored in literature at Cornell University before concentrating on psychiatry, had already published an extended study of one of Dostoyevsky's novels and was contemplating writing a book about Dostoyevsky when he realized he would have to understand something about the author's gambling in order to analyze the man and his work. To accomplish this, he began looking for a compulsive gambler to treat in his practice. One thing led to another, or, as he says, "I guess I got hooked."

"Even today," Rosenthal says, "Dostoyevsky's *The Gambler* is our best case history of a compulsive gambler. It is full of insights and a rare understanding of the problem. Yet it is autobiographical, written by a man who was obsessed by gambling and who remained so for years. In retrospect, I think it was the question of self-deception which intrigued me. With such seeming understanding, how could Dostoyevsky have continued to be so self-destructive?"

Rosenthal, who says his previous experience of treating patients with identity disorders and with a variety of impulsive or self-destructive behaviors was good preparation for treating compulsive gamblers, clearly enjoys being at a frontier in compulsive gambling where there are more questions than answers. In November 1989, in his office in a medical office building in the heart of Beverly Hills, he discussed the advances that have been made in our understanding of compulsive gambling and what remains to be done.

DISAPPOINTING RESPONSE

As he talked, a frustrating event was etched freshly in his mind. He had recently presented two workshops on compulsive gambling to the California affiliate of the American Society of Addiction Medicine, a group of 3,600 physicians and psychiatrists specializing primarily in alcohol and drug addictions, and had been somewhat disappointed with the outcome. At a panel discussion following his presentation, he says it was clear that those in attendance felt compulsive gambling belonged in the province of psychiatry instead of addiction medicine. "My presentation was well received, but I felt like the unwanted stepchild," he says. "The response of the addiction medicine folk was partly political, partly scientific, but largely a problem in education. It was political in the sense that having fought so hard to achieve some legitimacy in the eyes of the medical community, they were now defending their turf. They draw the line on addiction at substance ingestion (drugs, alcohol, even nicotine). They're also telling us that those of us in the gambling field are going to have to do our homework. We're going to have to talk about the effects of gambling on neurotransmitters, cognitive deficits, patterns of physiological withdrawal, and hereditary factors—that is, if these factors are there. It's healthy to be skeptical, but some of the other things said during the panel discussion surprised me. The doctors not only didn't regard compulsive gambling as an addiction, they didn't believe a Twelve-Step recovery program had any role in its treatment! One person clearly stated that if a Twelve-Step Program is effective for compulsive gamblers, that merely demonstrates the power of the program and that it would work for anything."

He continues: "When a hypothetical case was presented of a dually diagnosed alcoholic and compulsive gambler, the opinion was that the patient must first stop drinking. Then, after nine months to a year of abstinence—and only then—could he start dealing with his gambling and other life problems. Not one person in a room of approximately two hundred counselors and therapists who work in the field of alcohol and drug addiction questioned this."

Despite this experience and others like it, Rosenthal is hardly discouraged by the widely held attitudes about compulsive gambling. "Compulsive gambling is where the field of alcoholism was about thirty years ago," he says. "I guess that's one of those clichés everybody in the field trots out, but it's absolutely true. My own bias is that we will learn a lot about other addictions through working with compulsive gambling."

Although a psychoanalyst by training, Rosenthal is aware of the need to look at the physiological factors of compulsive gambling, as well as social and psychological factors. He is presently writing a paper with Henry Lesieur of St. John's University on the withdrawal phenomenon of compulsive gambling. He also is collaborating with colleagues at UCLA on a study of hyperactivity and pathological gambling.

Compulsive gamblers have been described typically as very energetic, restless, physically active people, and Rosenthal wants to see how this general condition compares to the psychiatric entity known as "attention deficit hyperactivity disorder." Based on the treatment of a number of "hyperactive" gamblers, he suspects there is a subgroup of compulsive gamblers "who begin gambling, not so much for excitement or action, but paradoxically, to calm themselves or slow themselves down." This same group may also use stimulants, cocaine, or amphetamines for the same purpose, he says, and "might clearly benefit from medication." Rosenthal predicts that someday soon, we will be able to classify gamblers into perhaps five or six subtypes, making treatment more effective. He says this is clearly what he is working toward.

BUILDING A NETWORK

Rosenthal also is deeply involved in the California Council on Compulsive Gambling, a nonprofit, voluntary organization made up of professionals in the field, recovering gamblers, and interested others. The purpose of the California Council and its parent organization, the National Council on Problem Gambling in New York, is fourfold: public education, research, prevention, and the promotion of treatment. The California Council is one of thirteen state affiliates of the National Council, and it came into being more or less out of necessity.

"After I treated my first compulsive gambler, and perhaps a couple of others, word got out that I knew something about compulsive gambling," Rosenthal recalls. "I began getting calls from the media and legislative assistants wanting information. When I didn't have what they needed, I'd try to get it for them or put them in touch with someone who could help them. This was how I discovered some wonderful people all across the country who were working with compulsive gambling: people like Arnie Wexler in New Jersey, who mailed me newspaper articles, interviews, and the results of early attempts at data collection. I'd run down to the copier place on the corner, and mail this information to others. Soon, a network of interested people began developing, and not all of them were back east. Some of the most knowledgeable were actually in California—like Julian Taber, Dewey Jacobs, and Nelson Rose. It was obvious how inefficient we were, working independently and duplicating each other's efforts, so founding of the California Council was inevitable."

Unlike other councils in New Jersey, Massachusetts, Iowa, and Minnesota, which receive state funding, the California Council relies solely on membership dues and volunteer help. Still it has been able to accomplish a lot in its three years of operation, including the establishing a state toll-free help line and becoming a clearinghouse for information. Rosenthal says that the California Council has also assisted communities concerned about gambling encroachment locally, has educated therapists, and has improved the spectrum of treatment and other services available in the state.

Despite the success of the National Council and its affiliates, resources in the field are meager. Rosenthal says foundations and other funding sources have been largely unsympathetic: "Gambling is not perceived as life-endangering, like alcohol or drug dependence. And I believe there is a taboo about money, and a special lack of sympathy for people who lose or appear to squander it." But he believes some major breakthroughs are imminent. "The Pete Rose case has generated intense public interest in compulsive gambling, and that should help immensely in terms of funding for research and education and strengthen participation in Gamblers Anonymous, both in California and elsewhere."

WOMEN AND GAMBLING

A strong GA program is essential for recovery, Rosenthal believes, but in Los Angeles, the birthplace of GA, only a couple of dozen meeting sites exist at the present, and none of the specialty groups that have proliferated throughout, can be found in GA. Until this past year, Rosenthal observed that not only was GA the least known of the Twelve-Step programs, but it appeared not to be growing at a time when legalized gambling and compulsive gambling were sharply on the rise. He is particularly concerned about the absence of GA meetings in California for Hispanics and Asians, two groups that he says are overrepresented among compulsive gamblers, and women, who frequently have a difficult time identifying with or feeling comfortable in male-dominated meetings. "We know that women make up only two to four percent of the GA membership nationally, and even less in California, yet they make up one-third of the compulsive gamblers."

Female compulsive gamblers are also underrepresented in treatment programs and private therapy, Rosenthal says. "As was the case with women alcoholics, the stigma is greater for female gamblers. We know that when a woman tells her spouse about her gambling problem, she is much more likely to be abandoned by him than when it is the other way around—when it's a male gambler acknowledging a problem."

Rosenthal says there are a number of differences between male and female compulsive gamblers. "First of all, a woman's choice of games is generally different. Women choose games that are less directly competitive, and which are based more on luck than skill. Secondly, women compulsive gamblers are more apt to be depressed and to gamble for escape, specifically to achieve an emotional numbing or oblivion. This is what they crave, rather than the action or excitement which the men are seeking. Women are less involved with a need to play the 'big shot' or impress other gamblers, and there's even less emphasis on the notion of a 'big win' as the solution to problems."

Rosenthal is quick to point out that these are generalizations and that there are many women poker players and men who are escape artists, but he says in looking at large numbers of compulsive gamblers, one cannot help being impressed by some of these differences. "Another difference between the sexes," he notes, "is in the development and progression of their gambling disorders. Women are much more likely to start gambling later in life than men. In fact, many of the women don't start gambling until they are already set in their adult roles. Men, on the other hand, start gambling early in adolescence, and are frequently out of control by high school. By that time, gambling has formed a very important part of a man's identity." Because they usually start gambling later in life, women gamblers "may be easier to treat," he adds.

KEY FACTORS

Like others in the field, Rosenthal is intensely interested in the question of why someone becomes a compulsive gambler. He rattles off seven factors which impress him as particularly important.

1. A family history of alcoholism or compulsive gambling. He says: "This need not mean that it is hereditary. It may indicate inconsistent parenting or neglect, a learned coping response, or an identification with the family member with an alcohol or gambling problem. This is an area obviously requiring a great deal of study."

2. Growing up in a family with an extremely critical, rejecting, or emotionally unavailable parent. "For men, it's usually the father," he says, "and there's a lifelong campaign to please that parent, and win his approval, which is generalized onto others as an overconcern with being liked or appreciated. There's a rebellion against this—a kind of pseudoindependence—as well as a great deal of destructive anger. Many compulsive gamblers grow up believing they can never be good enough, or they can never do enough. They develop compensatory fantasies of some spectacular success, like a 'big win,' which will show everybody just how good they are."

3. A family that emphasizes status and overvalues money. "The potential gambler is taught at an early age to equate money with self-worth," Rosenthal says, "or with power and control over people, or with security. For example, I've seen a number of compulsive gamblers among children of holocaust survivors, who grew up with fathers who were not only angry, depressed, or emotionally unavailable, but who believed that the only way to achieve security was to have enough money. This was their only way to counter a profound sense of helplessness and to assure themselves that what happened to them couldn't happen again."

4. Being brought up to be extremely competitive. "Compulsive gamblers typically are extremely competitive from an early age," Rosenthal says. "There are several reasons for this—some were deliberately raised that way, usually by their fathers. Winning became everything and since it was initially essential for parental approval, it was soon the basis for their self-esteem. [These gamblers] tend to think of themselves in all-or-nothing terms."

5. An early physical or developmental problem. "Those who are compensating for some physical or developmental problem which caused great shame and humiliation early in their lives may be at risk. This might include some congenital abnormality, a speech defect, a problem with bed-wetting, short stature, or delayed puberty."

6. Hyperactivity. "Gambling serves as a rather specific way to medicate oneself," Rosenthal says. "Just as some people discovered with video games or with certain drugs such as cocaine or amphetamines, gambling has a paradoxical effect—it slows them down, calms them, allows them to concentrate."

7. Exposure to gambling at a young age in a way in which it is particularly valued. "A number of compulsive gamblers identify with a parent or some important relative who gambled," he says. "Frequently they recall being introduced to gambling by them, how it was a shared activity and perhaps the only closeness they knew. A typical recollection was of father taking them to the racetrack. For others, there was a family card game, which they grew up watching. Being allowed to sit in was a sign of acceptance into the family or achievement of adult status."

Rosenthal says there are other factors, but any one or any combination of these seven descriptions can translate into a personality picture of the typical compulsive gambler. "Compulsive gamblers are often very energetic, highly competitive, restless, and easily bored. They frequently have a need to impress people, stemming from low self-esteem and an overconcern about being liked or appreciated. They may be generous to the point of extravagance—the big tipper or person who always picks up the check. When not gambling, they are often workaholics, although they may also be binge workers who wait until they are up against deadlines before cramming. Despite their general impulsiveness, compulsive gamblers view themselves as taking a long time to make decisions; procrastination is a major problem. Along with the need for approval, they are frequently thin-skinned, or overly sensitive. There's a tendency to think of themselves in all-or-nothing terms. Men who are compulsive gamblers are frequently good with numbers. Women tend to be lonely and depressed. Regardless of the type of gambling they engage in, both men and women seem to have more than the average interest in sports."

MORE RESEARCH NEEDED

Rosenthal cautions that not all compulsive gamblers fit this mode and that the general features he describes were gleaned from his experience as a therapist and from a survey he conducted with Henry Lesieur.

Rosenthal's southern California colleague Dewey Jacobs is also interested in predisposing factors in compulsive gambling and its development. He is focusing much of his current research on the onset of gambling in the teen or preteen years. Rosenthal says the release of Jacobs' 1988 study on teenage gambling and the lottery generated more interest in compulsive gambling in California than any single event to date other than the Pete Rose gambling case. We can conclude that more research and more attention to subsequent findings are needed. The Pete Rose case will soon fade out of mind and if compulsive gambling is to be recognized as a health issue with appropriate treatment indicated, then more disclosure of what is transpiring in the field is essential.

8

THE GAMBLING EPIDEMIC

For most of this century, the state of Texas was pretty much a member in good standing of the vast Bible Belt stretching across the old Confederacy. Time and time again in the 1960s and 1970s, with admonitions from the pulpits of the powerful fundamentalist churches tugging at their consciences, Texans went to the polls to cast ballots rejecting initiatives for the legalization of serving hard liquor in bars and restaurants and for pari-mutuel horse-racing.

The attitude of the electorate seemed to be that Texas was doing quite well, thank you, without revenue from sin taxes on alcoholic spirits and racetrack gambling. And who could argue with that? Throughout much of that long period, Texas enjoyed the fruits of its robust petroleum-based economy, which almost singlehandedly supported the state's public education system. Texas had no state income tax or sales tax, and most people figured that if anyone wanted to toss down a scotch or bourbon in a bar, or bet on the horses or dogs, they could always seek out an underground venue in the state or slip across the border to neighboring Louisiana, New Mexico, or Arkansas, or any of the dusty, anything-goes Mexican border towns scattered across an 800-mile stretch of the Rio Grande from El Paso to Brownsville.

Today, all of that has changed in Texas, in part because of the diminishing influence of conservative Protestant churches in a diverse, rapidly growing population, but primarily because of decreasing revenues and jobs in the once-mighty petroleum industry. Slowly but surely, a sales tax was approved, followed by a so-called "liquor by the drink" initiative, and some twenty years later, by pari-mutuel horseracing.

Transforming Texas

On November 5, 1991, the transformation of Texas reached full circle when voters defied strong opposition by state religious organizations and approved a state lottery by an overwhelming margin of 64 percent to 36 percent. The lottery, the thirty-fourth to be approved in the United States, is expected to generate some $800 million a year for the strapped state treasury by the 1993–1994 fiscal year. For the moment, the winners would seem to be the public programs that were on the budget chopping block if the initiative had failed, a few lucky people who will share the prize money, and the cottage industry of printers, advertising agencies, and merchants who will produce, promote, and sell the lottery tickets. The ultimate losers will be the bordering states, such as Louisiana, where Texans formerly flocked by the thousands to purchase lottery tickets, and the young, the poor (mostly minorities), and the elderly, all of whom inevitably may be tempted to spend more on the lottery than they can afford.

On election night in Texas, as it became apparent the lottery was passing, Weston Ware, a spokesperson for a Baptist group opposing the lottery, told the *Dallas Morn-*

ing-News, "Fantasy and delusion won today. The tens of thousands who play the lottery as a way out [of poverty] are the big losers. Those folks and their children are going to suffer."

None of the proceeds from the Texas lottery are earmarked for education, prevention, or treatment programs for problem gamblers. The opponents of the lottery won one small concession, however. The number of a toll-free telephone hotline for problem gamblers will be printed on each lottery ticket.

There were a couple of interesting sidelights to the Texas lottery story. First, the lottery hardly represented an avenue of last resort for raising revenues in the state. Texas is still one of the few states without a personal income tax. And, second, the leading supporter of the lottery initiative was Governor Ann Richards, a recovering alcoholic whose concerns about addiction obviously do not extend to the lottery. Governor Richards and other state officials apparently believed—and rightly so—that supporting a state lottery was far safer politically than supporting new taxes to cover revenue shortfalls. On election night, Governor Richards told the press, "I thought the people preferred the lottery to taxation, and they proved it at the ballot box."

DECREASING REVENUE AND INCREASING MARKETING

That's hardly a revelation, but Ann Richards and other supporters of the Texas lottery measure can easily be excused for embracing the lottery as an answer to their state's fiscal woes. They were simply following the lead of elected officials in thirty-three states, reaching all the way back to New Hampshire in 1964. Today, many of these same officials are trying to revive sagging lottery revenues by devising innovative ways to boost ticket sales. For example, California, which recently hired a new state lottery director, is considering instituting a series of games designed to produce daily winners and create what its new director terms a more "casino-like" atmosphere. Total revenues from the California lottery decreased from $2.63 billion in 1989 to $2.48 billion in 1990. Perhaps even more importantly, net income plummeted from $1.9 billion to $929.4 million, according to the magazine *Gaming & Wagering Business*. The same publication reported that five other states—Iowa, Kansas, New Jersey, Pennsylvania, and Washington—also posted sales declines from 1989 to 1990.

Wisdom and experience tell us that the type of games being considered by California and other states—more action-oriented games with frequent payouts—are more likely to appeal to compulsive gamblers than relatively passive games with odds as high as 23 million to 1. From a marketing perspective such a move would certainly make sense, since compulsive gamblers tend to spend many times more on gambling than the public in general. An apt comparison might be in the alcohol beverage industry, which sells an estimated 80 percent of its products to approximately 20 percent of the drinkers, many of whom are alcoholics.

New marketing considerations aside, state lotteries already have had a significant impact on the increasing incidence of problem gambling, as studies by Jacobs, Lesieur, and others have shown. Part of the increase is attributable to what Dr. Durand Jacobs describes as the pied piper effect of the lottery. He says the lottery introduces young people—and sometimes the elderly—to gambling and, once hooked, teenagers in particular quickly move on to other forms of gambling.

Brubaker believes the lottery poses a significant relapse threat for recovering compulsive gamblers. He knows of one case in which the purchase of a single one-dollar lottery ticket set off a full-blown relapse for a compulsive gambler. "It reactivated his gambling mind-set," Brubaker says, "and he began dreaming of striking it rich again. The lottery is very threatening to recovering gamblers because of the lure of big jackpots and its accessibility. There are lottery machines by the checkout counters in every supermarket and convenience store in California. That's just too tempting for a lot of people who are not really solid in their recovery."

For some, however, the lottery represents much more than a gateway to gambling or a relapse issue. The seemingly innocuous game with its ridiculously high odds is pursued by some problem gamblers with a fervor worthy of a high-stakes casino player or a racetrack or sports bettor.

ENTERTAINMENT OR GAMBLING?

This book focuses primarily on compulsive gamblers and their behavior, not gambling in general and the types of games gamblers play. Nevertheless, the lottery deserves a special look because of its accessibility and the fact that it is operated by the government and promoted as a form of entertainment rather than gambling.

Bingo, another distinctive, seemingly harmless mainstream form of gambling, also merits a look. Although bingo involves considerably more action than the lottery, particularly as it is practiced on the federal Indian reservations, both it and the lottery appeal essentially to the same audience—the poor, the minorities, and the elderly. The two games also have something else in common: people who play them to excess frequently don't acknowledge that they have a problem with gambling, and as a result, they don't seek help through Gamblers Anonymous or some type of therapy or treatment.

First, let's examine the lottery, which with the capitulation of Texas is now accessible to the citizens of the nation's nine most populous states—California, Florida,

Illinois, Michigan, New Jersey, New York, Ohio, Pennsylvania, and Texas.

When state lotteries first came into play, they were opposed on moral grounds and because they were a form of regressive taxation rather than because they were an open invitation to compulsive gambling. In fact, some experts on gambling problems didn't think the lottery would appeal to compulsive gamblers because it was a game of chance with astronomical odds and little, if any, action.

Despite lottery officials' protests to the contrary, the regressive nature of the lottery has been shown in study after study. A study in Michigan found that lottery sales were three times higher in low-income, inner-urban areas than in more affluent suburbs. A study in Iowa found that low-income groups spent up to nine times more on the lottery than did upper-income groups. The Michigan study further showed that in one low-income neighborhood in Detroit, the *average* household spent 6 percent of its gross income on the lottery.

Dr. H. Roy Kaplan's studies of lottery winners have yielded similar findings. Kaplan found that most winners came from what he termed "working-class backgrounds." In a 1978 study by Kaplan, none of the lottery winners had graduated from college, and nearly all were employed in semiskilled or skilled blue collar jobs. Later studies revealed that the average age of lottery winners was fifty-four, leading Kaplan to conclude: "As with the poor, the elderly are particularly susceptible to the lure of instant riches since many of them are on fixed incomes which often place them marginally above the poverty level . . . Since winners are representative of players, being randomly selected, this indicates the popularity of lotteries among the [older population]."

While the concerns about the regressiveness of the lottery proved to be warranted, gambling experts woefully underestimated the appeal of the game to compulsive gamblers. What they didn't bargain for was the sheer inventiveness and self-delusion of some gamblers. A surprisingly large number of lottery players believe they can greatly increase their chances of winning by picking from a list of hot numbers or by following other systems. It is precisely this group of players who form the ranks of compulsive gamblers among lottery fanatics, says Mike Brubaker.

"The big players pick their own numbers because it gives them a sense of power and control," Brubaker says. "And the bigger the jackpot the more they play. In a way, they create their own action—planning what numbers to pick, how much money they're going to put down, and so on. They are classic compulsive gamblers, but most of them won't admit it. They say they play the lottery for fun."

Following is a sampling of stories about lottery players, drawn from several sources, including the fine television documentary, "Gambling: Pushing Your Luck," produced by television station KQED in San Francisco. Although some of the people in these stories appear to fit the description of a problem gambler, only one admits to having a problem.

LOTTERY STORIES

Many Texans simply couldn't wait for the start-up of the lottery (sometime in the summer of 1992) in their state. They had been streaming across the Louisiana border in droves since September 6, 1991, the day the Louisiana lottery opened shop. According to the *Austin American-Statesman*, a small grocery store in southwestern Louisiana, just across the border from the Beaumont–Port Arthur area of Texas, sold 1 million "scratcher" tickets in the lottery's first six weeks of operation, making it the number one lottery outlet in the state. Most of the players were Texans—some from as far away as Houston.

Two women from Houston drove 200 miles round-trip to

buy about $200 worth of tickets each at the grocery store. Another man drove about 50 miles each week to purchase $100 worth of tickets. The man says the trip is cheaper than going to Las Vegas, which indeed it is. But the odds are much better in Vegas. The odds of winning a $5000 or $10,000 prize in the Louisiana lottery are approximately 50,000 to 1. One of the bigger players from Texas—a middle-age woman—rejects the contention that the game preys on the poor, and another is quick to point out that while she spends well over $100 on her trips across the Sabine River into Louisiana, she is always sure "not to go overboard."

All the Texans at the Louisiana store said they were counting the days until the start-up of the Texas lottery.

In a particularly poignant episode of "Gambling: Pushing Your Luck," the KQED documentary, Dr. Valerie Lorenz, executive director of the National Center for Pathological Gambling in Baltimore, leads a woman addicted to the lottery through a withdrawal exercise over the telephone. Lorenz, one of the nation's foremost experts on treating lottery players, has asked the woman to call her with the numbers she wants to play in the lottery as a substitute for actually laying down money to purchase tickets. Lorenz, who estimates that approximately 10 percent of the compulsive gamblers she encounters have a problem with the lottery, describes the process she is going through with the caller as "mind betting." She says the exercise is just one small first step in helping the woman quit gambling.

The woman on the other end of the line is deeply in debt from losses sustained in the lottery, and she frequently goes without food to save money to play. She began playing the lottery compulsively after scoring a fairly big win. The woman has agreed not to gamble while undergoing counseling by Lorenz and says she hasn't played the lottery in about a week.

As the drama unfolds, the woman appears to be experiencing a rush from reeling off her numbers to Lorenz in rapid-fire succession. Once the exercise is complete, the woman announces that she feels better. "After I place the bets, I feel okay," the woman says shortly before signing off.

Minutes later, the phone rings in Lorenz's office. It's the woman calling again. She admits that she was lying—that the telephone exercise was merely a charade. The woman bought eleven lottery tickets and won forty-five dollars. She had been watching the lottery drawing on television and checking her numbers against the winning numbers as she talked with Lorenz. She apologizes to Lorenz, but says: "You see, I do win. I pick 'em when I play, and I pick 'em when I don't play."

When the woman hangs up, Valerie Lorenz looks dejected. "Oh, dear," she says softly.

Mike Brubaker tells of two men in California who borrowed $10,000 each and pooled their money to buy 20,000 Lotto 6-53 tickets when the jackpot in that game reached more than $100 million. The men won a total of only $2,400 in prizes, leaving them with a loss of $17,600. For the same drawing, a man from the Midwest organized a syndicate of investors who put up $2 per ticket and flew to California to buy $45,000 worth of lotto tickets on behalf of the syndicate. The only winner in the scheme, Brubaker notes, was the man who formed the syndicate. He grossed almost $45,000. The investors weren't discouraged, however; they plan to make similar group purchases in other lotteries when the jackpot exceeds a preset amount.

Although he buys about five dollars worth of lottery tickets per week, a drugstore clerk in a large eastern city breezily dismisses any notion that he has a problem with gambling. He says he plays the lottery as a diversion and reserves his serious gambling for regular monthly trips to Atlantic City. He also frequents a nearby racetrack.

When playing the lottery, the thirty-five-year-old clerk,

who describes himself as one of the working poor, uses an intricate system for selecting numbers based on how often certain numbers turn up as winners. He usually increases the number of tickets he buys when the jackpot rolls over. He considers himself a winner when he picks at least four of the six winning numbers correctly, even though the prize money for four correct numbers rarely exceeds his outlay for the week. He believes a win of that type validates his system.

Once, when he was strapped for cash a couple of years ago, he sat out a week, and sure enough, five of the numbers he would have selected were drawn. He figures that episode cost him over a thousand dollars, so he hasn't missed another lottery drawing since, even when he's been forced to borrow or skip bill payments to stay in the game. One of the payments he skipped was a support payment to his ex-wife, who had him hauled into court.

He says confidently that sooner or later he's going to win big in the lottery.

Dramatic cases of lottery abuse are rare in comparison with other forms of gambling. One reason is that the people who play the lottery usually don't have big sums to lose. Perhaps the most dramatic example to date of a lottery player run amok was that of a young Michigan housewife who was convicted of writing bad checks and forging money orders to support a $1,000-a-day lottery habit. Over a period of eighteen months, the young woman reportedly lost between $250,000 and $300,000 playing the lottery.

A Safe Bet

Even those losses pale, however, in comparison with those of high rollers such as Alex Petros, Pete Rose, or television sports producer Chet Forte, all of whom lost in the millions of dollars. Alex Petros recalls playing the California lottery only once—when the jackpot soared past $50 million for the first time. He went into a liquor store to buy a package of cigarettes and on impulse bought $400 worth of lottery tickets. Later that night he became bored with the process of checking his numbers against the winning numbers to see whether he had won and ended up getting someone else to check the tickets for him. He never played the lottery again.

Ironically, one of the big winners in the early days of the California lottery was a friend and former employee of Alex Petros. She is a young mother of two and a waitress at a San Francisco restaurant Alex formerly owned. When the lottery first started in the mid-1980s, the woman and her husband, who is a house painter, began buying about ten dollars' worth of lottery tickets a week, and about six months later, she won a trip to Sacramento for the "Big Spin," a wheel-of-fortune type game which is televised live to whip up excitement about the lottery. The young woman won $2 million, which at that time equalled the biggest prize paid out by the California Lottery. Unlike a compulsive gambler, the young woman set her husband up in his own contracting business and socked most of the money away for her children's education and retirement. She still works in the same restaurant six years later.

"Imagine that," Alex says with a laugh. "She saved most of her winnings. I probably would have gambled it all away."

Two-million-dollar jackpots, of course, are something the great majority of lottery players only dream about in idle moments. Most players buy a ticket or a few tickets from time to time, or on a regular basis, check the winning numbers to see how they fared, and simply go about their business when they lose, which they almost always do. For some players, however, the lottery is a burning obsession as alluring as the games in the great casinos of Las Vegas or Atlantic City. Without doubt, the lottery is rapidly becoming the game of choice for compulsive gamblers who don't have access to other forms of gambling or who can't afford to play high-stakes games. Within a year or two after the start-up of the Texas lottery in 1992, the number of compulsive gamblers in that state will increase substantially, just as it did in thirty-three other states previously.

The growth of bingo into a high-stakes, casino-like game is even more perplexing than the lottery explosion. For many Americans, the very mention of bingo evokes memories of sweet little old ladies playing bingo cards at community fundraisers and church socials. For Catholic churches, in particular, bingo fundraisers have provided a major source of support for church schools and athletic teams. *Newsweek* reports that some Chicago parishes raise $40,000 a year or more on bingo games to support Catholic elementary schools and that the New York archdiosese raised more than $11 million in 1985 from bingo, bazaars, and other events. Sociologist William McCready of the University of Chicago told *Newsweek* that bingo "is as Catholic as an Irish wake or a Polish wedding."

B - I - N - G - O

Contrast that old-fashioned, Norman Rockwell-like image with that of some churches' and charities' practice of hiring professional gambling promoters, who command up to 40 percent of the gross proceeds to run weekly and nightly bingo games in giant halls that produce millions of dollars a year in revenue. And contrast that further with the vast multimillion-dollar bingo operations that have sprung up on federal Indian reservations throughout the United States. These big games are about as far removed from church socials as sandlot baseball is from the World Series, and they are becoming increasingly accessible to more

Americans as Indian nations from Oklahoma to Minnesota to California seek to bolster their standard of living and provide badly needed jobs on the reservations by operating gambling operations there.

As if to underscore the appeal and money-making potential of bingo, the game is becoming increasingly popular in casinos in Las Vegas and other Nevada towns that cater to lower-end gamblers. The Showboat Hotel and Casino in Las Vegas runs what it calls the "highest stakes bingo game in Nevada," with daily payouts of up to $150,000. Palace Station, the Horseshoe, and the Holiday Inn in Las Vegas and Harrah's and the Riverside Casino in Laughlin, Nevada, all operate fairly rich games around the clock. And then there is the annual $40,000 World Championship Bingo Cruise out of Miami, sponsored by *Bingo Bugle,* a national newspaper with regional editions which is distributed free of charge at most major bingo establishments. The entry fee for the on-board bingo is $200 per person, plus fares of from $980 to $2,080 for the cruise.

For the moment, however, the leading bingo venues are on the Indian reservations dotting America. *USA Today* reports that the Jackpot Junction Casino on the Lower Sioux Reservation in Minnesota is served by airline tours from twenty-one cities and attracts 150 charter buses a week. In a span of only two years, the casino, which is located in southern central Minnesota within easy driving distance of residents of five states, has grown from a simple bingo parlor into the largest casino between Atlantic City and Las Vegas. In addition to its huge bingo room, it has 1,100 slot machines and forty-four blackjack tables. The casino grosses about $20 million a month, and profits from its operations have enabled the Sioux to establish scholarship and home loan funds and build a sparkling new community center.

Other successful bingo operations on reservations include those of the Creek Nation in Oklahoma and the Chitimacha in Louisiana. The Creeks operate five bingo halls, which attract approximately 50,000 visitors a year and net more than $3 million for the tribe. The bingo halls also provide meaningful employment for some 225 Creeks. Further South, about 1,200 people pay a forty-five-dollar admission fee every Saturday night to play high-stakes bingo at the new $2 million bingo hall on the Chitimacha Reservation near Franklin, Louisiana. Each winning card in the Chitimacha game pays $1,000, and the total payout is about $40,000 per night. The Chitimacha, like the Creeks, pour most of their revenues back into the community for health care, education, and social services.

Business Week estimates that in 1989 as much as $350 million was wagered on bingo and other games on some 120 of the 310 federal reservations in the contiguous United States. Some of the bingo operations are linked together via satellite for a game called MegaBingo, which offers nightly jackpots of $10,000 and a chance at a $500,000 jackpot. Gamma International, Ltd., which operates MegaBingo, estimates that $60 million was wagered on MegaBingo in 1990—more than double what was bet a year earlier.

Since most of the profits from bingo go toward worthwhile projects, both on the Indian reservations and in communities and churches, there is little strong opposition to the proliferation of legal bingo games. Some Catholic clergy do object, however, to the reliance of some parishes on revenues from bingo and other forms of gambling for support. Bishop Warren Boudreaux of Louisiana, an opponent of bingo, told *Newsweek* in 1986 that supporting the church through playing bingo lacks the unselfish generosity demanded by the Gospel since the player, in effect, expects something back. Chicago's Cardinal Joseph Bernardin told the same magazine that he was appalled by heavy betting at parish "Las Vegas nights" and thought there must be better ways than bingo to meet the social and financial needs of the church.

Some politicians are also concerned. Minnesota Attorney General Hubert H. Humphrey III told *USA Today* that he was concerned about the explosive growth of gambling in his state. "We need to halt the expansion of gambling, take a deep breath . . . and let the regulatory end catch up," Humphrey said. There are currently ten casinos on Indian land in Minnesota.

There certainly can be little doubt that with the advent of high-stakes games and greater accessibility, bingo has become a popular game for problem gamblers, many of whom are women. While the fast-paced action and casino-like atmosphere of bingo appeals strongly to some men, women gamblers are more likely to be attracted to bingo because it is essentially a game of chance, requiring no handicapping skills and little, or no, knowledge of odds.

BINGO STORIES

Women players, most of them middle-aged, were clearly the majority for a regular Saturday-night session in the fall of 1991 at the Morongo bingo hall, one of three large bingo operations on Indian reservations near the California desert resort city of Palm Springs.

About one thousand people had gathered in the large bingo parlor off a busy interstate highway to play for more than $20,000 in prize money. They had arrived by car and by buses and vans operated by the bingo parlor, and they were seated at long, rectangular, Formica-top tables lined up in neat rows on the floor of the mammoth football field–size building. Most of the players remained seated throughout the long night except for occasional trips to the snack bar or restroom, giving the room the orderly, well-organized appearance of a giant classroom. Only players were allowed in the game area, and they were tactfully discouraged from table-hopping once the games began. Alcoholic beverages were prohibited in the building and on the property.

In the rear of the giant structure was an elevated, partially enclosed stage that served as the nerve center of the operation. From the stage, announcers read aloud the numbers selected for each play and later verified the numbers on winning cards, which were hustled to the stage by runners working the tables. The runners responded instantly when a player shouted, "Bingo!" When a bingo was verified, an official on stage counted out the prize money in cash for the runner to carry back to the winning players. The process was fast-paced and precise as it unfolded under the watchful eyes of dozens of security guards and supervisors on the floor and in glass-enclosed offices above the playing area.

Many, if not most, of the employees in the bingo hall were members of the Morongo tribe, and most of the players were white, middle-class women, some in their sixties or seventies. The crowd also included a large number of Hispanic men and women. The players who arrived by bus were from as far away as Santa Monica, about 100 miles to the west, but most, including those who came by van, were from the immediate area. One woman told about a popular bumper sticker in the area that read: "Keep Your Grandma Off the Streets: Support Legalized Bingo."

The regular games that night began at seven o'clock, preceded by a warm-up session at six fifteen and so-called "late bird" games beginning about eleven thirty and lasting until a little past midnight. Admission was twenty-five dollars, which entitled each player to two pads of bingo cards for the eighteen-game regular session. Warm-up and late-bird cards cost extra, as did additional cards for the regular session and cards for several jackpot games, including the $500,000 MegaBingo game, which was televised live via satellite. Prizes for each game in the regular session ranged from $1,000 to $2,000.

• • •

Real Action

The games themselves were like a mosaic, with winning patterns in the shapes of *Xs*, *Ls*, *Ts*, *Zs*, Indian stars, solid blocks of six and nine squares, two-layer cakes, three-layer cakes, kites with tails, large diamonds, broken picture frames, spiders, and so on. The patterns were flashed on two large electronic tote boards at the beginning of each game, primarily for the benefit of novices. Veteran bingo players know the patterns by heart, much like expert card players know every variation of poker or blackjack.

The real action, however, wasn't on the stage, or on the tote boards, or in the type of game being played. The real action was supplied by the players themselves.

The regulars set up shop prior to the start of each day's play. They bring bingo paraphernalia with them in cloth bags or briefcases, along with snacks, good luck symbols, crossword puzzles, seat cushions, reading material, astrological forecasts, and whatnot. One woman carefully placed framed photographs of her family on the table in front of her, and another woman produced a photo of her winning a $2,500 jackpot at another bingo establishment in the area. Both said the photos were for good luck.

The prized possession of every serious player in the house was his or her "daubers," a set of oversized multicolored ink pens used for marking the bingo cards. The daubers come in different sizes and shapes. There are designer daubers, which make brightly colored marks in the shapes of hearts, four-leaf clovers, and stars; hammer daubers, which are shaped like their namesake and are reportedly easier to handle; and holiday daubers, with marks in the form of Christmas trees, bells, and so forth. The dauber inks come in bright, transparent colors that are easy to see, but don't obscure the number underneath. Most players treat their daubers with care and respect, much like golfers do their golf clubs.

When play began, the daubers became a blur of pink,

blue, green, magenta, orange, and red as the players furiously marked their pads of cards as each number was selected. Rather than listen for the announcer's call of the number (B-1, I-16, N-31, G-46, O-61), the regulars stay focused on television monitors placed strategically on the floor. The monitors display pictures of the small white plastic balls bearing the numbers several seconds before the numbers are announced over the speaker system.

It is easy to separate the pros from the amateurs. While novices struggle to keep up with the eight bingo cards per game that are part of the standard admission package, the regulars easily play two to three times that many cards. The pros play with an economy of motion, sitting with their markers posed as they check the monitors for the numbers and then quickly recording the numbers on their cards, which are laid out in neat rows in front of them. One woman who plays at least once a week says it takes only a matter of seconds for her to play each number on twenty-four cards. "The trick is learning exactly where to look on each card and cutting out any unnecessary movements," she says. "It takes practice."

Most of the regulars know each other. They generally play at the Morongo hall during its regular business hours on Friday, Saturday, and Sunday, and may move on to other games in the area on the average of once or twice a week. In the past, most if not all of the regulars have won significant jackpots of several hundred dollars or more. For some, that big win was what got them hooked on the game.

TOMORROW'S GOING TO BE A LUCKY DAY

A woman we'll call Betty is typical of this group. She plays three nights a week at the Morongo game and usually ventures out on Tuesday night to play in a lower-stakes game at a high school near her home. She says that if she didn't win occasionally she would have quit playing long ago. She hasn't won a jackpot in a few months, and she admits that her periodic wins don't come close to covering her playing expenses. "Bingo is my social life and hobby," she says. "Most of my friends are people I've met playing bingo."

Betty, who is in her sixties, has played cards and bingo since she was a youngster growing up in Detroit. She and her husband, who was a construction worker, moved to California in the 1960s and almost immediately developed a passion for Las Vegas, which they would visit two or three times a year. Betty would usually play the slots, while her husband, Jack, shot craps or played blackjack.

Jack died suddenly eight years ago, leaving Betty a home that was paid for and a small union pension. Betty, who had never held a regular job, lives off Jack's pension and Social Security, both of which total up to about $1,200 a month. She spends more than $100 a week, or about a third of her income, on bingo, and says that is well within her budget because her expenses are low. "My daughter [who lives in the San Francisco area] complains about me playing so much, but I tell her it's none of her business—it's my hobby. She worries that I don't eat right or take care of my health. That's nonsense. I'm healthy as a horse."

Betty has been playing at the Morongo bingo hall since the day it opened, approximately seven years ago. "The people who work here are like family to me," she said as she packed up her belongings after the last game on Saturday night. She had been shut out again, but one of her friends had won $500, splitting a $1,500 jackpot with two other players. Betty will be back at her favorite table near the snack bar in a few hours for the Sunday matinee session.

"I miss coming here on the days they aren't open," Betty says. "I get bored staying home and watching television. I would play every day if I could. I guess I like playing the slot machines in Las Vegas or Laughlin as much as I like bingo—but that's not convenient for me and the people who run the big casinos aren't like family. For me, the ideal would be to open up real casinos on the Indian reservations. I think everybody around here is in favor of that."

Betty says that through the years she has known several regular players who spent more on bingo than they probably should have. She stopped far short, however, of acknowledging that they were compulsive (or problem) gamblers. "One woman I knew lost her house because she couldn't pay her bills, and she finally quit coming around. I don't think bingo was her problem, though. I think she just didn't know how to manage her money."

Betty dreams of winning a large jackpot, but says that isn't what keeps her coming back to the bingo tables. "I won two thousand dollars once, and I spent it all on bingo and a trip to Laughlin. The money's not important to me. I like the excitement of playing and seeing that last number I need come up on the screen. [Bingo] takes my mind off everyday problems, and gives me something to look forward to."

As she begins to make her way out into the cool night, Betty exchanges good-byes with a security guard and one of the floor supervisors, both of whom call her by name. Near the front door, she pauses and observes: "I can hardly wait until tomorrow. My horoscope says tomorrow's going to be a lucky day for me."

9

A LIFELINE

In 1987, Tom Finney, a prominent forty-five-year-old union official on the West Coast, checked into a motel near his home, scribbled out a short note to his children, put a gun to his temple, and pulled the trigger. He died instantly.

The suicide stunned Finney's friends and colleagues. The dashing, handsome union leader appeared to have an earlier drinking problem under control; he was at the height of his career; he had a new girlfriend, a new car, and a new luxury apartment. He had appeared to be as outgoing and carefree as ever as he cut a wide swath in political and union circles throughout his sphere of influence. Yet when Mike Brubaker learned of Finney's suicide, he wasn't overly surprised, and in the days that followed, it became apparent why. According to the handwritten note left at the scene of the suicide, Finney was drowning in a sea of debt and had fallen hopelessly behind on his support payments to his first wife. Later, some irregularities in the finances of the union local, which Finney headed, would be discovered.

Finney was a compulsive gambler and on that fateful night in the fall of 1987, after returning home from a trip to Las Vegas, he had taken what he thought was the only course available to him—a bullet to the brain. "I had heard he was gambling heavily and living a lavish life-style," Mike says, "but he wouldn't let anyone get close to him. Tom was too arrogant to get with the 'program.' "

The program to which Mike Brubaker refers is the program of Gamblers Anonymous, which has been the salvation of thousands of compulsive gamblers like Tom Finney. Finney had attended GA meetings on a few occasions, but for reasons known only to him, he rejected it. His rejection was strange because Finney had faithfully attended Alcoholics Anonymous meetings in the three years since he had quit drinking and the Twelve-Step Program was familiar to him.

Had Tom decided that GA was for him, he would have met many others in the GA fellowship who had once considered ending it all with a bullet, a bottle of pills, a razor blade, or a one-car automobile crash. Various researchers have found rates of attempted suicide among compulsive gamblers to be as high as 25 percent. Of a group of GA members surveyed by the late Dr. Robert Custer, more than one out of three said they had experienced strong suicidal thoughts. All of them, however, said that their lives had improved considerably since they began attending GA meetings on a regular basis.

On a Saturday in 1989, a burly outdoorsman from out of state sat anxiously near the door leading into a long rectangular room at Charter Hospital of Las Vegas. His left arm was in a sling. He wore the look of a man who had been to hell and back, which in fact he had. A few days earlier, while in the throes of a deep depression over gambling debts and what he perceived as his abject failure in life, he had inserted a loaded shotgun into his mouth, braced himself, and pulled the trigger. Incredibly, the gun misfired and exploded backward into his left arm.

COMPANY OF STRANGERS

The horrifying experience had devastated Milt Langley, who was writhing in pain and sobbing uncontrollably when he was found by a man who had responded to the loud bang made by the backfire of the faulty shotgun. Stricken in his agony, Milt Langley received a reprieve. Within hours of his aborted suicide attempt, he agreed to seek professional help after spilling out the details of his gambling to his family.

At the suggestion of a hometown physician, Milt's family contacted Charter Hospital of Las Vegas and accompanied Milt on a flight to Las Vegas. He was admitted to the compulsive gambling treatment program at the facility. Charter's compulsive gambling program was until 1990 the only one of its kind west of Montana. On his first full day at the hospital, he was seated in an armchair among a group of about twenty-five people in the warm, comfortable, group therapy room decorated with clusters of paintings of desert scenes hung on the off-white walls.

Milt Langley's condition had been very unstable upon admission to the hospital, but after a night's sleep he was ready to participate in his first meeting at Charter Hospital. A stranger to virtually everyone in the room at that Saturday meeting, Milt found himself with six people he would come to know well.

The leader of this meeting was not a psychologist or even a former patient of the hospital. He was a sturdy, straightforward man named Al who identified himself as a compulsive gambler at the opening of the meeting and noted that he had made his last bet eighteen years ago. Al said he owed his recovery from compulsive gambling to the program of Gamblers Anonymous.

It was the regular Saturday noon meeting of GA at Charter Hospital, and it was open to all compulsive gamblers in the community, including Charter patients. It was the first such meeting Milt Langley had ever attended. There are no

GA meetings in the relatively small town where Milt lives, much less a hospital treatment program for compulsive gambling.

Milt would discover in the days ahead that at least five people in the room with him that Saturday had attempted suicide. In fact, a man in his thirties who was seated across from Milt had attempted suicide four times before finally being admitted to the hospital for treatment. The man noted with a laugh that either he wasn't very good at killing himself, or he really wasn't serious about committing suicide in the first place. Milt, of course, had not been so ambivalent; he had clearly intended to end it all.

The group gathered for the Saturday GA meeting was a diverse mixture of people. About a third of the group were women, and most, with the notable exception of the leader, Al, had been in GA for less than a year. Among the group was a young poker dealer at one of the casinos in town; a buxom woman in her late twenties or early thirties with long, flowing hair; a Protestant minister from out of state; a well-dressed local accountant with several years of abstinence from gambling who was attending this meeting for the first time; a former airline flight attendant with an intense interest in gambling problems among women; a demure housewife; a woman from England who had just learned that her estranged brother had died in London earlier that week; and an upbeat businessman from the Midwest who was returning home the next day after completing a three-week stay in the hospital.

Al ran the meeting with a gravelly voice and the precision of a drill sergeant. He recited the preamble of GA to open the meeting and reminded those in the room that "what's said in this room stays in this room." He also advised the group that he would tolerate no crosstalk during the meeting. Before proceeding with the rest of the meeting, Al announced that the group had a special order of business to discuss. A visitor wanted to sit in on the meeting and since this was a closed meeting (for compulsive gam-

blers only), the request required the unanimous approval
of the group. Al courteously explained that a negative vote
should in no way be construed as a rejection of the visitor
personally and asked the visitor's forbearance in the matter. No one objected and the meeting resumed with a series
of readings by individuals in the group from a book called
the "combo book" of Gamblers Anonymous. The readings
included recitals of the Twelve Steps of Recovery for GA
(which are virtually identical to those of AA) and the
Twelve Traditions of the GA Unity Program (which focus
heavily on anonymity).

Al then reeled off a few announcements about GA activities in the area and urged those in the room to seek the aid
of the GA's Pressure Relief Group if they were experiencing undue pressure from financial, legal, or other matters.
He gave out the telephone number of the leader of the
Pressure Relief Group, a man named Jerry C., whom Al described as a skilled financial advisor and recovering compulsive gambler.

The Pressure Relief Group is one aspect of GA that sets it
apart from AA and the other self-help groups. Pressure Relief Groups are composed of recovering compulsive gamblers who assist newcomers to GA with their legal and
financial affairs, which are usually in a state of total disar-
ray. Working from a financial inventory provided by the
newcomer, the group sets up a budget including a repay-
ment schedule for debts and requires that the newcomer
report back to group periodically as to whether he or she is
adhering to the plan.

The Pressure Relief Group is not for the fainthearted,
and many newcomers shy away from it—often to their
detriment. Gamblers seeking help from the Pressure Relief
Group are required to contact all creditors and ask for a
thirty- to forty-five-day moratorium on payments, to choose
someone to handle their money, to turn over all ownership
of properties (including their car) to someone else, to re-

move their names from all bank books, checking accounts, and credit cards, and to turn over all paychecks (uncashed with the stub attached) to the individual who will manage their money. The group also advises the newcomer whether legal counsel may be necessary to address illegal acts committed during the course of gambling activity.

The Saturday group leader, Al, had sought help from the Pressure Relief Group and today he swears by it.

The first part of any self-help group meeting is generally referred to as the housekeeping portion of the meeting. What follows is the heart and soul of the Twelve Step experience. In AA, it's a process called sharing. GA calls it therapy.

A silence fell over the room at Charter Hospital when Al began laying out the ground rules for the therapy part of the meeting. Some people began fidgeting and averting their eyes from Al as he spoke. No one wanted to be the first to speak. Al announced that the therapy session would be limited to one hour and asked each person to confine his or her remarks to two or three minutes so everyone could participate. Some GA meetings permit cross-comments if a person wants feedback on his remarks, but this meeting was far too large for that. Cross-comment meetings are open-ended affairs that sometimes last two or three hours.

As the silence deepened, Al looked searchingly around the room for volunteers. Finally he said, "If no one wants to go first, I'll begin calling on people." With that, a brunette to Al's right broke the silence. She recalled how she had first come to the GA program several months earlier after she had become hopelessly addicted to video poker in Las Vegas. After she finished speaking, others began chiming in one by one and the mood of the meeting rose noticeably. Some stories evoked laughter and others brought out shouts of encouragement or congratulations.

THE FIRST STEP

Throughout the entire process, Milt Langley sat self-consciously tugging at the sling swaddling his left arm. Al never once glanced at Milt when there was a lull in the action. It was clear that he didn't want to push Milt. Near the end of the meeting, after nearly everyone had spoken, Milt straightened up in his chair, raised his right hand tentatively to get Al's attention, and said, "I'm Milt and I'm a compulsive gambler. This is my first meeting and I'm glad to be here." The group responded "Hi, Milt," and Milt began unraveling the story about his attempted suicide. Milt looked straight ahead as he talked and spoke with great difficulty. Gradually, though, his voice gained strength. He began to make eye contact with others as he told them about the depth of his despair arising from mounting losses at racetracks, high-stake poker games, and weekend gambling forays into northern Nevada where he tried to get even at the casinos. He said he wanted to "get a handle on things in treatment and make up for the pain" he had inflicted on his family. He concluded by thanking everyone for listening and sank back into his chair with relief.

When the meeting ended a few minutes later, Al and the others in the front of the room quickly made their way over to Milt and offered encouragement. Soon those in the back of the room began streaming by. Milt, a large man with chiseled features, seemed slightly embarrassed by all the attention, but he managed a smile for the first time before leaving the room to go next door to sign in for his medication at the nurses' station. He left the room much more at ease than when he had entered ninety minutes earlier.

Milt had taken the first step most recovering gamblers take in the journey toward recovery—attending a GA meeting. It's a process that first began with the founding of GA in Los Angeles in 1957 by a recovering alcoholic known as Jim W. Unfortunately, most of those who begin the journey

fail, at least in the beginning, but those who, in the GA par-
lance, "keep coming back" for days, months, and years
seem to succeed in overcoming their compulsive gambling
problem.

The treacherous road to recovery is best illustrated by
the fate of the founder of GA. Jim W. resumed gambling after a period of abstinence and quit again only when his
health failed. He died in 1983 at the age of seventy-one at a
rest home in Los Angeles.

Yet the program Jim W. started has helped tens of thousands of compulsive gamblers recover. In his introduction
to the "Blue Book," which serves as the bible of GA, the late
Dr. Robert Custer noted, "Compulsive gambling is treatable
and Gamblers Anonymous has been and is the single most
effective treatment modality for the pathological gambler . . . GA is effective because it undercuts denial, projec-
tion, and rationalization; identifies the serious implications
of gambling; demands honesty and responsibility; identifies
and corrects character problems; gives affection, personal
concern, and support; develops substitutes for the void left
by the cessation of gambling; and is nonjudgmental. The
more a person understands Gamblers Anonymous, the
more one respects and admires it for its principles, accomplishments, and effectiveness—and the lives it has saved."

Milt Langley completed the treatment program at Charter Hospital of Las Vegas and returned home in December
of 1989. At last report, he was attending GA on a regular
basis at a meeting about 40 miles from his home and has refrained from gambling.

Las Vegas might seem an unlikely spot to recover from a
gambling problem, but Dr. Robert Hunter, the clinical director of the compulsive gambling unit at Charter Hospital
of Las Vegas, says it is, in fact, one of the best places because
of the tight-knit GA network in the city. There are from
three to five GA meetings a day in Las Vegas or twenty-
seven meetings a week at eleven locations in all. This com-

pares to thirty-three meetings a week in the vast Southern California area stretching from Los Angeles to San Diego. Because of the availability of meetings, Dr. Hunter frequently recommends to his out-of-state patients that they set up temporary residence in Las Vegas following treatment at the hospital to reinforce their recovery through attendance at GA meetings. Hunter, a protégé of Dr. Custer, firmly believes that heavy involvement in GA offers the best guarantee of recovery for compulsive gamblers.

Fortunately, the number of GA meetings in the United States and throughout the world is on the rise. GA's International Service Office in Los Angeles reports that about one hundred new meetings have been started in the last year, bringing the worldwide total to about fourteen hundred, eight hundred of which are in the United States.

Certainly scenes such as the one described at Charter Hospital of Las Vegas are no longer unusual. Similar scenes are played out daily in churches, synagogues, schools, restaurants, hospitals, walk-up offices, community meeting rooms, and in self-help clubs established by GA members. These self-help clubs are not sanctioned by GA since one of its traditions prohibits GA from owning property "lest problems of money, property, and prestige divert us from our primary purpose."

TURNING ONE'S LIFE AROUND

GA—like its older, more established counterpart, AA, which was founded in 1935—is a remarkable organization by any standard. Its International Service Office or headquarters is tucked away in a small, rented sixth-floor office suite in a building above a parking structure near downtown Los Angeles. Its literature and other materials look more like church bulletins and high school newspapers. The yearly budget for operations at GA's headquarters, including salaries and rent, is $133,000, most of which dribbles in a few dollars at a time from the contributions collected at individual meetings and from the proceeds of literature sales and conferences. In short, GA is simply the mom-and-pop operation that its founders had in mind when they adopted the GA Unity Program based on the Twelve Traditions of AA. The Unity Program is designed to keep GA free of outside influences, controversy, and internal organizational issues so it will remain focused on its "primary purpose [of carrying] its message to the compulsive gambler who still suffers."

The International Executive Secretary at GA's International Service Office in Los Angeles is an enthusiastic, friendly, forty-three-year-old Los Angeles native known to outsiders by her first name only, Karen. She is a compulsive gambler with ten years of recovery who left a higher paying retail job in May of 1989 for her post with GA. "I used to bet on anything and everything," Karen says. "I love my job. I can't believe they pay me to do what I do. I wouldn't go back to my old job for any amount of money. I work with many of my friends and really appreciate life today. I have a peace of mind now that I never had before. While I was gambling, I spent my whole life on the run."

Karen is one of only two full-time paid employees who share the three-office GA suite. GA employs one part-time employee who comes in as needed to help out with mailings and other office tasks. The only other help is a group of volunteer recovering compulsive gamblers who pitch in with office duties and with answering the phones, which are constantly ringing.

The phone is the centerpiece of the office. In between orders for publications and requests for information, staff and volunteers alike are on the alert for calls from compulsive gamblers in need of help. These calls are the lifeblood of GA. The office refers callers with gambling problems to nearby GA meetings or arranges for a recovering gambler to visit with the caller. These visits are referred to as

"Twelve Step" calls after the twelfth step of the GA program, which implores recovering gamblers to "carry the [GA] message to other compulsive gamblers." During these visits, which frequently occur late at night, a recovering person shares his story with the gambler in distress and explains how GA can turn one's life around.

TWELVE STEPS

Karen and her staff—and the thirty GA intergroups around the country—maintain lists of recovering gamblers who have expressed an interest in making Twelve Step calls. Other recovering gamblers make regular Twelve Step calls to prisons, jails, and hospitals.

The twelfth step is the critical service link for the growth and survival of GA. The first eleven steps of the GA program focus on personal growth and recovery.

The steps of the GA program are:

Step 1: We admitted we were powerless over gambling—that our lives had become unmanageable.

Step 2: Came to believe that a power greater than ourselves could restore us to a normal way of thinking and living.

Step 3: Made a decision to turn our will and our lives over to the care of this power of our own understanding.

Step 4: Made a searching and fearless moral and financial inventory of ourselves.

Step 5: Admitted to ourselves and to another human being the exact nature of our wrongs.

Step 6: Were entirely ready to have these defects of character removed.

Step 7: Humbly asked God (of our understanding) to remove our shortcomings.

Step 8: Made a list of all persons we had harmed and became willing to make amends to them all.

Step 9: Made direct amends to such people wherever possible, except when to do so would injure them or others.

Step 10: Continued to take personal inventory and when we were wrong, promptly admitted it.

Step 11: Sought through prayer and meditation to improve our conscious contact with God as we understand Him, praying only for knowledge of His will for us and the power to carry that out.

Step 12: Having made an effort to practice these principles in all our affairs, we tried to carry this message to other compulsive gamblers.

Although the twelve steps of the GA program differ only slightly from those of AA, the people in GA are quick to point out that their program is not just a carbon copy of AA. Karen, of the International Service Office, notes that GA members are urged to rely on GA literature instead of AA literature because of the different nature of their problem. She says, "All self-help groups are good, but gamblers need GA because we can identify with each other's problems. That's what makes our program work."

Most of the identifying takes place at individual meetings where compulsive gamblers meet on a regular basis to share their stories, their fears, and their innermost feelings. Most GA regulars have a home group that they attend at least once a week. Generally, their sponsor or mentor in the program and any people they sponsor all attend the same meeting and a deep bonding, which sometimes lasts a lifetime, occurs.

A number of recovering compulsive gamblers in the Greater Los Angeles–Orange County area call a one-story stucco house in a Hispanic section of Anaheim their home. The small house has been converted into a club for GA and Gam-Anon, a recovery group for family members and others close to a compulsive gambler. Overeaters Anonymous also uses the clubhouse. The club, which is known as the Orange County Self-Help Center, hosts at least one GA meeting a day, sometimes two. Members can choose from a total of nine meetings a week, including a spaghetti dinner meeting for GA and Gam-Anon members on Saturday night. Forty to fifty people usually turn out for the joint GA–Gam-Anon meeting and attendance at the other meetings ranges from a handful at the Sunday night cross-comment meeting to about twenty to twenty-five for the meetings which are open to compulsive gamblers and others who wish to attend.

The club was formed by a group of about twenty GA members in 1986 because there was a scarcity of meetings in the burgeoning Orange County area south of Los Angeles. Sally Jackson, one of the charter members of the club, says, "There just weren't enough meetings in the area and we thought we needed a place where people could find a meeting every day of the week."

The club currently has about fifty-five members who pay dues of ten dollars a month—or $100 each a year—to support it. The dues don't cover the rent of $600 a month and the utilities, so the club has fund-raisers such as dinner dances, breakfasts, and garage sales to make up the difference. The members handle the upkeep of the property. "Everything we have is a result of contributions. We've put down a new carpet, taken out a wall to make a meeting room, and furnished and equipped the house with donations," says Sally, a friendly woman who serves as a kind of den mother for the club. "Our next project is to paint the outside of the house. We'd like to be able to buy the house eventually, but right now, we're just content to make the rent and have a regular place to meet. It's very difficult under any circumstances for someone to recover from compulsive gambling and if you can't find a meeting, it's even harder. I owe my life to Gamblers Anonymous. I want others to have the same chance I had."

10

SALLY'S GAME PLAN

T ime. She would never leave the table to eat, preferring instead to munch on the sandwiches the house brought around periodically. She rarely excused herself to go the bathroom, which only served to aggravate her health problems.

"I was a total mess," Sally says, "but I couldn't quit playing. I didn't feel the pain while I was playing—only after. They would have to pick me up and carry me to my car when I was ready to leave. My legs were so swollen I couldn't walk or stand up straight. But I would be back the next night if I was able. I sometimes would come in on crutches or in a wheelchair, but I always came back."

Sally's game was a card game called panguingue, or pan for short. It's played with eight decks of cards minus the eights, nines, and tens from each deck. Pan and other games such as pia gow are popular at card clubs in California and at casinos. Unlike poker, the action is fast-paced and heavy, much like craps.

Sally played pan at two-card clubs near her home in Anaheim. The city of Anaheim has since outlawed card clubs, but other cities in the Los Angeles area have picked up the slack. The small town of Gardena, south of downtown Los Angeles, has several large clubs and Commerce, an industrial city just a few miles east of downtown Los Angeles, has a glittering new club resembling a casino, which is clearly visible from the busy Santa Ana Freeway leading into Los Angeles.

The clubs are havens for compulsive gamblers in the Los Angeles area. They gather at the clubs in between trips to Nevada and sit for hours at a time playing cards at tables with other serious gamblers. At virtually any GA meeting in the Los Angeles area, card players usually outnumber other types of gamblers by as much as 2 to 1.

CHASING A LOSS

The clubs are not for the casual card player. Some are dark gymnasium-like places on the interior where grim, highly skilled players, some of whom are professional gamblers, compete for each other's money instead of the house's. The house's take comes from renting spots at the tables, and from food, drink, and credit, which is easily obtained.

The card clubs in Anaheim were Sally Jackson's entire universe when she was gambling. "All of my social activities were there," she says. "I didn't have any friends outside the clubs and rarely spent any time with my family." Sally, in fact, was on the payroll of the clubs as a prop. "A prop is the gambling version of a prostitute," Sally says with a laugh. "My job was to sit down at an empty table to get a game going. I propped six days a week and was always on call in case the action slowed down at the club. On the other day of the week, I was a manicurist."

The club, however, usually didn't have to bother calling Sally. She was often there two or three days running, playing pan on her own time as well as the club's time. Sally knew she was in trouble with her gambling, but despite numerous attempts to quit, she always returned to the clubs. And each time she returned, her gambling increased even more.

Once she managed to stop gambling for a period of one month, but found that she was even more depressed than when she was agonizing over her problem with gambling. "I had no self-worth or self-esteem, and at times, I just wanted to die," she recalls. "The only time I felt any self-worth is when I was gambling. I got caught up in the excitement of gambling, and all of my troubles just seemed to disappear—even if I was losing. Winning or losing really didn't seem to matter anymore. But the minute I stopped gambling, I felt terrible physically and mentally and was so worried about money that I couldn't sleep. I was so much in debt that I was afraid I was going to lose my house, and if I did, I knew that would be the end for me. My house was the only worldly possession I had left."

Sally played on credit at the clubs and was constantly borrowing from friends, banks, and finance companies to cover markers. "I was getting paid by the club, and I won a lot of the time," she recalls. "But when you're betting a thousand dollars a day and 'chasing' to try to cover losses, you're always going to end up losing in the long run. I never could get up a winner, like my ex-husband could. From the very first time I gambled, I played until all of my money was gone."

Sally's last gambling binge began a week before Thanksgiving in 1978 and lasted six straight days. She didn't change clothes during that time and rarely left the table. She finally left the club the night before Thanksgiving, slept fitfully for a few hours, and drove from Anaheim to Los Angeles for Thanksgiving dinner at her daughter's.

While she was driving back to Anaheim, Sally was overcome by an intense desire to return to the club. She wanted to win back her losses of the previous six days to cover her markers and make enough to pay off a $1,200 bank loan which was due on Monday. She stopped at four places where she regularly cashed checks, but all of them were closed because of the holiday. When she reached home, Sally was in a panic. But instead of going to the club to try to wrangle more credit, she reached for the phone and called Gamblers Anonymous. "I don't know what I expected," Sally recalls, "but I was desperate and needed to do something. I had been to a GA meeting once before to see what it was like, but had never gone back. I didn't see GA as a solution to my problem. I thought I should be able to quit on my own if that time ever came."

Sally dialed the GA number and received a recorded message that listed a series of numbers to call. She got no answer on the first two calls, but on the third, she reached a man named Jim.

Sally began pouring out her story to Jim, but he cut her short, asked for her address, and told her he would be by in a few minutes to pick her up for a GA meeting in Paramount about 20 miles away. Sally burst out crying.

"I couldn't believe what I was hearing," she recalls. "Here was a man who didn't even know me, who was going to leave home on Thanksgiving Day to pick me up and drive me to a meeting a half hour away. I couldn't stop crying. I couldn't believe anyone would care that much."

THE BEGINNING OF A BETTER END

Jim came by as scheduled, and Sally Jackson's life was transformed. She hasn't made a bet or stepped inside a card club since. Sally attended the Paramount meeting and a meeting every day or night for the next year.

She quickly found a sponsor, a long-term recovering gambler named Phil who is still her sponsor today. Over the course of Sally's first year in GA, Phil guided her as she worked the Twelve Steps of the GA Recovery Program and encouraged her to reach out to others.

Sally recalls that her first moment of truth in Gamblers Anonymous came on the Monday following Thanksgiving when her $1,200 note was due at the bank. "Jim and Phil told me to go to the bank on Monday and request an extension on my loan. I had never done anything like that before since I had started gambling. I was always borrowing from Peter to pay Paul, or chasing my losses at the card clubs. I was scared to death to walk into a bank and ask someone to renew my loan. I sat in my car outside the bank for about an hour trying to get up the courage to go into the bank. I thought I couldn't go through with it. I thought maybe I should just forget GA and go back to the club to try to work something out. I knew I could always count on this one friend in a pinch.

"But I thought about what Phil and Jim had told me and how relieved I had been when Jim had said he would pick me up to take me to that meeting. Finally, I worked up the nerve to go inside about fifteen minutes before the bank closed. They renewed my loan. I paid a fee, and left—simple as that."

In Sally Jackson's mind, the event at the bank marked her first realization of the full power of the GA program.

Today, Sally Jackson epitomizes success in GA. In addition to helping start the Orange County Self-Help Center, she sponsors seven people on the GA program and personally attends two or three meetings a week. She also is available day or night to respond to Twelve Step calls, as Jim did for her on Thanksgiving Day of 1978. She says unequivocally that GA "saved my life" and that she feels a great need to help others with gambling problems. Sally says she has grown immensely in her eleven years of recovery.

"I feel much better about myself today," she says. "I have quality people in my life; I'm there for my family; I'm helping other people; and I'm not wasting my time worrying about getting money or paying my bills. It's been a total turnaround for me."

Sally's obsession with gambling began on her first trip to Las Vegas in 1952 and lasted another twenty-six years. She went to Las Vegas on her honeymoon and immediately fell in love with the great casinos in the southern Nevada city that was beginning to boom from gambling and a glittering nightlife.

"I was a fierce competitor in marbles and jacks when I was a kid, but I had never gambled for money before that trip," Sally recalls. "My husband was a gambler, and we spent a lot of time in the casinos while we were there. I was hooked almost from the first moment I played a hand of cards in the casino. It was exciting and glamorous and fun—everything that had been missing in my life up to that point."

Living Proof

Sally had never felt close to her parents while she was growing up in the Los Angeles area and recalls feeling unloved. Her parents never showed affection to each other or to their three children. Sally recalls one particularly painful scene when she was sixteen. The family was planning to celebrate the end of mortgage payments for their house, but instead a violent argument erupted between her parents, and her father beat her mother within earshot of the children. The argument began when Sally's father came home and announced to his wife that he had lost his paycheck playing poker.

Sally says her father lost his paycheck gambling several times, but she doesn't recall his ever being addicted to gambling like she was. She says the same was true for her husband, to whom she was married for more than twenty years before they were divorced in 1976.

"My husband was a heavy gambler, and as far as I know, he's still gambling," Sally says. "But he could always get up and leave a game when he was winning. I never could do that. He also had a gambler's mentality. He always tried to keep up appearances, no matter how strapped we were for money. He spent ten thousand dollars landscaping the yard in front of our house in Van Nuys, while on the inside our floors were bare. We bought and sold houses, went through bankruptcies, had cars repossessed—everything. But my husband always wanted to look good on the outside."

Even though Sally herself was a heavy gambler, she nevertheless badgered her husband about his gambling throughout most of their marriage. "He was our breadwinner, and he just lost, lost, and lost," she recalls. "He was a public accountant, and once during the peak tax season, I stopped by his office to see if I could help out. The office was closed, and I found him in a card club in Gardena. I stormed in there, made a big scene, and cut off his credit at the club. I don't recall ever contrasting his behavior to my own. That's part of the insanity of compulsive gambling: you don't see yourself as you really are." While her husband was spending his time in the card clubs of Gardena, Sally was frequenting another club about 30 miles away from Gardena on the outer edge of the San Fernando Valley. She would pack her daughters off to school and head off for a panguingue club in a white house with a small sign out front. The club had only eight tables and was located just a few miles from Sally's home in the heart of the San Fernando Valley.

"That's when pan came into my life," Sally says. "I never could seem to get enough of it. I would always stay longer and gamble for more money than I had intended. I missed a lot of car pools, and a lot of valuable time with my daughters. But I was drawn to that club like a magnet. My whole life seemed to revolve around the club."

Sally also made frequent trips to Las Vegas with her husband or with girlfriends from the club. She always played cards in Vegas. "I was never interested in dice or horses or anything else," she says. "Cards were my game, especially pan."

After her daughters were grown, and she and her husband were divorced, Sally dispensed with all pretenses of a normal life and became plugged in full-time with the clubs in Anaheim, where she had moved following her divorce. She bought a house with the settlement from the divorce and lived off her alimony and her pay as a manicurist and a prop at the clubs.

"I had no life whatsoever other than playing cards during the last two or three years I gambled," Sally says. "If it had been possible, I would have gambled around the clock every day of the week. When I wasn't gambling, I was lonely, depressed, and didn't care whether I lived or died."

During her first years of recovery from compulsive gambling, Sally substituted Gamblers Anonymous activities for her gambling, and says she has only recently begun to broaden her social circle.

"It's not easy for a single woman to recover from compulsive gambling—particularly a woman my age," she says. "The retention is very poor in Gamblers Anonymous, especially for women. I don't think women gamblers are as sociable as men, and it's hard for us to become involved in all the activities like parties, golf, ballgames, conferences, and the like.

"A woman has to work extra hard at the GA program, especially when you have a lot of free time on your hands like I do. But I'm living proof that single women can recover, and I believe more and more of us will in time."

WOMEN:

LOST IN THE SHUFFLE

In the fall of 1988, Mary Lou Strachan, a University of Nevada–Las Vegas criminal justice student, sat in the back of a large meeting room at the Golden Nugget Hotel in Las Vegas and listened to speaker after speaker recite studies and statistics about compulsive gambling. She was attending the third annual conference of the Nevada Council on Compulsive Gambling. She was fascinated with the presentations, but near the end of the program, it began to dawn on her that not a single statistic about female gamblers had emerged from the conference.

Mary Lou's interest in the subject was more than casual. She was not there in her role as a student. Instead, she was attending as a patient from the compulsive gambling treatment unit at Charter Hospital of Las Vegas. Mary Lou was a compulsive gambler who, only a few nights before, had written an $800 hot check, which she knew she couldn't cover, so that she could continue feeding dollars into video poker machines at a neighborhood gambling establishment in Las Vegas.

Mary Lou was bewildered and humiliated by her gambling compulsion. Like most people, she thought that heavy gambling was primarily a male domain, which only added to her feelings of guilt and shame about her addiction. Following the conference, Mary Lou asked Dr. Robert Custer, a consulting psychiatrist for the Charter program and a speaker at the conference, whether any studies had been done on female compulsive gamblers. He replied that to his knowledge there were none.

After her discharge from treatment, Mary Lou Strachan began a study of female compulsive gamblers in Las Vegas. Dr. Custer helped her design a questionnaire to be completed by women in Gamblers Anonymous in Las Vegas. Even though Mary Lou had no prior research experience, she plunged headfirst into the project in consultation with Custer and Dr. Robert Hunter of Charter Hospital.

During a nineteen-day period in March 1989, she visited fourteen GA meetings in Las Vegas and collected fifty-two completed questionnaires from women attending the meetings. She then inserted the numbers in the computers of the University of Nevada–Las Vegas and helped Custer analyze the data. Almost a year to the day when the question about female compulsive gamblers first entered Mary Lou Strachan's mind, she presented the results of her survey at the fourth annual conference of the Nevada Council on Compulsive Gambling. The presentation took place in the same room where she had sat in the audience as a patient only twelve months earlier.

Mary Lou Strachan, a petite, high-energy, forty-three-year-old former airline flight attendant with short-cropped blonde hair, laughs about the instant celebrity she achieved as a result of her survey. She has been quoted in newspapers and has appeared on PBS and ESPN television specials on compulsive gambling. She says, "That goes to show how hard up we are for research on compulsive gambling. Here's a person with one year of recovery from compulsive gambling and no prior research experience being treated like an expert on female gamblers."

All humor aside, Strachan and Custer's survey on female compulsive gamblers, however limited, is deeply disturbing. Sixty-nine percent of their respondents said they had contemplated suicide (compared to 36 percent in Custer's survey of a predominantly male group of GA members); 36.5 percent said they had embezzled or stolen money from their employer to support their gambling habit; and 10 percent said they had resorted to prostitution to obtain gambling money.

Obviously, some of the numbers may have been skewed by the fact that the survey was limited in its scope and was conducted in Las Vegas, where, for instance, prostitution is quasilegal. Still, the study seems to confirm that women are attracted to solitary games (as Dr. Richard Rosenthal hypothesizes), and that women may be more prone than men to be depressed and suicidal over their gambling.

A DISTURBING PROFILE

Strachan and Custer asked the women in their sample 106 questions on topics covering their gambling habits, family history, and mental and physical health history. The gamblers they surveyed fit the middle-class American stereotypical mold. The majority of the women were white, in their thirties or forties, were currently married, had one or more children, and were presently employed. The only obvious anomaly was that almost half the women surveyed were employed or had been employed in the gaming industry. The overwhelming game of choice for the women surveyed was video poker, and most of the women played in casinos. Most of the women said they had been gambling compulsively for more than two years prior to joining GA, and about three out of four said they had been in the GA program less than a year and were attending one to four meetings a week at the time the survey was taken.

During the course of their gambling activities, most of the women said they had written bad checks, had raided the family savings account, had sold jewelry or other valuables to obtain cash, and had borrowed money from parents, relatives, their spouse, or friends to pay gambling debts. One-fourth of those surveyed said they had declared bankruptcy as a direct result of their gambling.

The family history of the female gamblers was particularly revealing. Forty-two percent of the women said one of their parents gambled too much, and another 42 percent said one of their parents was alcoholic. Nearly one-third of the women said they had been physically abused by their parents as a child, and more than one-fourth said they had been sexually abused as a child.

Approximately one-tenth of the women said they were alcoholic, almost one-fourth said they had been addicted to illegal drugs, and one-seventh said they had been addicted to prescribed medication. Most of the women said they had suffered from depression, had consulted a psychiatrist or psychologist, and had contemplated suicide. Twenty-three percent said they had actually attempted suicide.

Less than half of the women surveyed knew that compulsive gambling was classified as a mental disorder, yet all of the women met the diagnostic criteria for the disorder. A sizeable percentage of the women surveyed (34.2 percent) reported that they had abstained from gambling for less than thirty days, and only six of the fifty-two in the sample reported they had been abstinent three or more years.

Mary Lou Strachan is quick to admit that her survey may be reflective only of Las Vegas female gamblers, but she hopes that at the very least it will stimulate more research into female compulsive gambling. She and others interested in compulsive gambling suspect that the incidence of compulsive gambling among women may be higher in Las Vegas because solitary forms of gambling, such as slots and video poker machines, are easily accessible. Gambling may also be much more socially acceptable for women in Las Vegas than in other parts of the country.

These facts would seem to be borne out by attendance at GA meetings in the city. Whereas Sally Jackson was the only woman in a group of twelve at a recent GA meeting in California, the ratio of women to men at Las Vegas GA meetings is usually 1 to 1, or better. "The women at most GA meetings here outnumber the men," Mary Lou says.

THE VIDEO POKER PHENOMENON

One thing is for certain about Mary Lou Strachan's survey: the surveyor fits the profile of the gamblers she studied. Like forty-five of the fifty-two women who completed her questionnaire, Mary Lou was what she terms a "video poker addict."

Even though she can't support her opinion scientifically, Mary Lou is convinced that video poker may be the most addictive game ever devised, and she fears that more and more women—and men—will become addicted to the game as its popularity continues to spread. "I had no intention of doing a survey on women gamblers myself when I first met with Dr. Custer. But I told him I was really interested in the video poker phenomenon," Mary Lou says. "He said if I was interested in finding out about video poker, I should do a survey. He said he would help me, and that got me really enthused. I suspected most of the women in GA were addicted to video poker, but I wanted to find out for sure."

The video poker phenomenon was even more pervasive than Mary Lou had imagined. Only seven of the women surveyed were addicted to any form of gambling other than video poker, and five of those played other machine games—slots and video keno. None of the women surveyed selected blackjack, craps, sports betting, or horse racing as their game of choice.

Mary Lou also discovered that four out of five women had a special machine or two they always tried to play and 84.6 percent said they normally "loaded up" their machine, or played the maximum amount of coins allowable. The places the women played varied: nearly half the women played in casinos near their homes, one-sixth played in grocery stores or drugstores, and two women played in laundromats or convenience stores. About half the gamblers played quarter machines, and the other half played dollar machines, and when they played, they tended to do so for long stretches. Seventeen women played seven to twelve hours at a stretch, thirteen played thirteen to eighteen hours, and eleven played twenty-five hours or more.

Interestingly, more than 40 percent of the women surveyed said they agreed with the statement, "I would not have become a compulsive gambler if video poker and keno machines had not been invented."

"The survey confirmed my suspicions, and a whole lot more," Mary Lou says. "Conducting the survey was a wonderful opportunity for me, and I believe it helped me solidify my recovery."

Until she was introduced to video poker, Mary Lou Strachan was a self-described social gambler. She and her husband, who is an airline pilot, moved to Las Vegas in the mid-1970s, but despite the lure of the casinos, she gambled only occasionally—maybe once every three or four months.

Mary Lou had another problem, though. She was an alcoholic.

In 1980, after quitting her job of fourteen years as a flight attendant with a major airline, Mary Lou slipped into a life of idle drinking while her husband was out of town on trips. She found that she was bored much of the time, and that drinking helped relieve her boredom.

Her drinking problem became progressively worse until December 1985, when she finally sought help. Stopping drinking seemed to transform Mary Lou's life. She decided to begin a new career and enrolled at the University of Nevada–Las Vegas to complete a degree she had begun working on twenty-two years earlier at the University of the Pacific in Stockton, California. Her major was criminal justice, and she quickly became a stellar student, posting a 3.74 grade point average.

On the way to her degree, however, she encountered video poker.

A F O R T Y - D O L L A R Q U A R T O F M I L K

"School kept me busy at first," Mary Lou recalls, "but when my husband was gone, which was quite often, I would get very bored and lonely. I had too much time on my hands."

To fill her time, Mary Lou began going to a neighborhood casino with her friends to play slots and video poker. She played sporadically in the beginning, but in 1987, she hit a big jackpot, then another, then another. In a period of a few weeks, she hit eight jackpots worth $38,000. She was hooked.

"I was hypnotized by the video poker machine from the very start," Mary Lou says, "but that first big win was what really set me off. I couldn't believe the sensation it gave me. I knew I would never be bored again."

Within a year, that $38,000, plus another $12,000 in a joint savings account, was gone. Mary Lou played three quarter and dollar machines on a daily basis at the casino where she hit her first big jackpot and began playing at the grocery store where she did her shopping.

"Our grocery store has fifteen video poker machines, and I would find any excuse I could to go to the store," Mary Lou says. "I would write a forty-dollar check to buy a quart of milk and pour all my change into the machines. It was like I was paying forty dollars for a quart of milk. After I stopped gambling, I didn't go to the grocery store by myself for three months."

After her jackpot winnings were gone and she began dipping into the family savings and borrowing money from friends, Mary Lou finally confided in her husband about her gambling problem.

"My husband was very supportive and understanding," she says. "He said he was willing to do anything he could to help me. I felt better, but the obsession was still there. I thought I could stop on my own, though. I didn't want to hurt my husband any more than I already had. I was doing fine in my recovery from alcoholism, and I thought that might see me through the gambling thing."

She was wrong.

In October of 1988, during her last semester of college, Mary Lou Strachan went over the edge in her gambling. While her husband was out of town on extended flying duty, Mary Lou caved in to her compulsion to gamble despite having promised that she wouldn't gamble while he was gone.

"I went insane," Mary Lou says. "I rushed over to my favorite casino and began playing as fast as I could. I remember getting a two-hundred-dollar line of credit, a four-hundred-dollar cash advance on my credit card, and writing two checks that I thought I could cover. When all that money was gone, I drove to another casino and wrote an eight-hundred-dollar bad check that I knew I couldn't cover the next day. I lost the eight hundred dollars in six hours. Then the reality of what I had done hit me."

Mary Lou doesn't remember driving home from the casino. She was sick to her stomach and frightened, and her thoughts were clouded not only by the current events in her life, but also by memories of her mother and of her mother's suicide, which had taken place years ago. When she reached home, Mary Lou sank into a chair by the telephone. It was late on a Saturday night, and she was exhausted and scared. But as she sat there crying in the dark, something clicked in the back of her mind about a doctor at Charter Hospital whom she had seen on television talking about compulsive gambling. She flicked on the light, found the doctor's name in the telephone book, and called him. A crisis operator, who recognized the panic in Mary Lou's voice, kept her on the line while she patched her through to the doctor. The doctor was Charter Hospital's Rob Hunter.

"I remember Rob talking gently to me to calm me down," Mary Lou says. "He said, 'You are going to be all right. You have a disease, and we can do something about it. I want you to drive to the hospital so we can evaluate your situation.' I did as he said because I really couldn't think of anything else to do. I was like a zombie. I thought I was the only person in the world with a gambling problem like mine."

COMING CLEAN

Mary Lou was admitted to the hospital and assigned to the compulsive gambling program that is part of the hospital's alcohol and drug treatment unit. She was in a deep state of depression and was filled with remorse and guilt. "I remember thinking I couldn't stand to face my husband," she says. "I felt like I had betrayed his trust in me and wasn't worthy of another chance."

Mary Lou just went through the motions in the treatment program for the first two days. She was the only gambler in the program at the time she was admitted and had difficulty adjusting to the alcohol and drug patients since she herself had been sober for almost four years.

Finally, though, Hunter began to break through to her in one-on-one therapy, and she came clean for the first time about the amount of money she had lost gambling. "That's a key issue with us gamblers," she says. "Because of all the lying and hiding we've done, it's very difficult for us to own up to how much money we've lost. We always try to minimize our losses. Once I got honest about that, I was able to open up in group therapy and in one-on-one. My husband took part in the family treatment program and in some of the group sessions, and once again, he was very understanding and supportive."

Mary Lou turned all of the family finances over to her husband while in treatment, and even today, she carries only $1.50 in cash with her. "Just enough for a pack of cigarettes," she says with a smile.

A year into her recovery, Mary Lou still attends three self-help meetings a week and has become a regular around the hospital as a result of her research work. She completed her B.A. in criminal justice shortly after being released from the hospital, but as of November 1989, she was too involved with her gambling research project to look for work in her chosen field. "I'm just letting things happen in their own time," she says.

Her husband, meanwhile, attends Gam-Anon meetings and continues to be very supportive of Mary Lou's recovery and her research work. "I'm very lucky to have my husband's support," Mary Lou says. "The stigma for female gamblers is terrible. I know of three women whose husbands filed for divorce while they were still in the hospital for treatment. Because the stigma is so bad, women are probably even more protective of their anonymity than men." On her part, Mary Lou is not concerned about her anonymity. "If I were," she says, "I wouldn't have undertaken the research project. I think recovering women need to step forward so other women will know they are not alone with their problem."

Mary Lou says that in many ways her recovery from gambling has been much more difficult than her recovery from alcoholism. She says that within three months after she had stopped drinking, she felt comfortable in a bar or restaurant that served alcohol. Even when she was gambling compulsively, with liquor being served all around, she says she never once considered drinking.

"I don't know why it's different," she says, "but I feel somehow that the urge to gamble is stronger than the urge to drink. I think about gambling constantly, and I won't dare go near a casino. The other day I was with some girlfriends of mine, and they decided they wanted to go to a casino to have dinner and play some blackjack. They said, 'It shouldn't bother you, Mary Lou, because you never played blackjack.' I told them, 'Thanks, but no thanks, I'll see you later.' People just don't understand."

Mary Lou says, however, that she believes people will understand in time as more becomes known about compulsive gambling. "Right now," she says, "I think people understand male gamblers better than females, but I think some good research on female compulsive gamblers will help change that."

THE COMPETITIVE WOMAN

Obviously, not all women gamblers are alike. Barbara Cummings, for one, would hardly fit the profile of the solitary, female compulsive gambler portrayed in Mary Lou Strachan's survey. She is a successful fifty-one-year-old, single woman who loved to mix it up with the men in high-stakes poker and who was at one time the highest-paid female executive in a giant international investment firm.

Gambling almost cost Barbara her job, but today she is a credit manager with the same firm and leads a much simpler life-style in a San Francisco Bay suburb, where she shares a Victorian house with another woman who handles Barbara's financial affairs. Barbara salvaged her fifteen-year career with her company by agreeing to undergo treatment in Maryland for compulsive gambling in the fall of 1986. She hasn't gambled since.

Barbara is not what you would term a dyed-in-the-wool Gamblers Anonymous member, but she does attend GA meetings on a somewhat regular basis and tries to adhere faithfully to the Twelve Step principles of the program.

Two weeks after the October 1989 earthquake rocked the San Francisco area, Barbara ventured a few miles south from her home to attend the Western Conference of Gamblers Anonymous in Sunnyvale and to share breakfast with her friend and confessor, Mike Brubaker, who had driven over from Monterey.

GA conferences are places where old friends in the program gather to catch up on the news with one another and to sit in on day-long meetings and glean some wisdom from high-caliber GA speakers. The conferences, which attract people from all over the United States, are open to members of GA and Gam-Anon, as well as to outsiders. About two hundred people, mostly from California, registered for the Sunnyvale conference, which was probably a good turnout considering the fact that the area was still being buffeted by aftershocks from the earthquake and many roadways damaged by the quake were closed.

Barbara Cummings drove to Sunnyvale with her housemate, Becky, a nongambler, to sit in on a couple of morning meetings before motoring back home in the afternoon. Her main reason for coming, however, was to see Brubaker, whom she had met in her early days of recovery at the recommendation of a hospital counselor.

Barbara was struck by Mike when they first met over coffee in Long Beach. "I couldn't believe anyone could have so much time [eight years] in recovery," Barbara says. "I hung on to every word he said to me. He was a ray of hope. He told me that I was going to get better and that life would go on. I felt like Mike was someone I could really talk to." The two have seen each other on a periodic basis since, as Barbara has shuttled between assignments in the East, Southwest, and West, and they talk frequently by phone. "Mike let me know when we first met that he was always available to talk, and I've taken him at his word," Barbara says. Mike said later he was pleased with how much Barbara had grown in her recovery since he had last seen her and commented on how well she looked. "She's still got a few resentments to work through," he said, "but I think she's doing real well."

Barbara Cummings' story is a dramatic rags-to-riches tale that almost ended as a full-blown tragedy because of her out-of-control gambling.

She grew up poor in a home with an alcoholic father in Louisville, Kentucky, the oldest girl in a family of eight children. The family moved twenty-two times in Barbara's seventeen years at home. She recalls the family living in a three-room flat across from a brewery, in which the five kids who were still at home were packed into one bedroom. She remembers that all she wanted out of life at that point was one more bedroom so she could have a little privacy.

Barbara's mother helped support the family by working as a waitress, and at the age of eight Barbara was left in charge of caring for the younger children. Barbara doesn't remember her father being sober for more than two months at a time, but says he was a very warm, loving man when he wasn't drinking.

She recalls becoming aware of the fact that her father was a sick man when she was only six or seven. She began caring for her father while her mother was at work and resented her mother "for not doing more to make him better." Her father eventually died of alcoholism.

"It was a terrible existence," she says, "and I really never outgrew it even when I became successful. I didn't feel I had done anything to deserve success. I always had this fantasy that I was going to lose everything and wind up being a bag lady. And I damned near did."

FAMILY TREE OF ADDICTION

Barbara's brothers and sisters haven't fared as well as she. She says only two of her seven siblings are not "currently practicing an addiction of some type, and I'm the only one in the family who has ever gone through any kind of treatment." Two of her brothers are compulsive gamblers as well as alcoholics, another brother is a compulsive gambler, and two of her sisters are alcoholics. The addictions extend to yet another generation. Two of Barbara's nephews have already developed gambling problems.

"Addiction pervades our family," she says, "and who knows when or if it will ever end." Barbara certainly won't be passing it on to another generation. She has no children and has never been married. To date, the only long-term relationship she has had was with a married man in New York. "I have had great difficulty with intimacy," she says. "The only type of relationship I've been comfortable with is one in which I take care of someone, like I did with my father. I always thought that to get what I wanted from people I had to take care of them."

Her father's alcoholism turned Barbara away from drinking. "I vowed I would never let what happened to my father happen to me," she says. "I view alcohol as a poison and don't use it. It never occurred to me until much later that people drank to mask pain."

Barbara was a high achiever from a very early age. She escaped home whenever she could to visit a nearby recreation center. She went all out in the activities at the center and soon attracted the attention of the staff, who arranged a scholarship for her at a private Catholic girls school in the city. The recreation center was her salvation, Barbara says; without it, she probably never would have risen above her meager beginnings.

Although Barbara thrived academically, attending the private school presented problems for her. "I felt like I was living in two worlds, and it was totally confusing," she says. "I was always acting out my confusion. I couldn't accept authority, and it seemed like I was always trying to screw things up." Barbara, however, felt secure at the school and eventually decided that she wanted to be a nun in the order that ran the school. The order initially turned her down because of her problem with authority, but after teaching for two years in the school, she was accepted back in the order as a provisional.

"I had felt like a total failure when I was rejected by the order the first time," Barbara says, "and I was determined to succeed the second time." Barbara took a vow of silence, worked hard at the teaching assignments she was given in different cities such as New York, St. Louis, and Los Angeles, and did her best to please her superiors. After four years, though, she was summoned back to the mother house and told she should leave the order.

"The Mother Superior said they thought that I would never be able to submit fully to authority and that I ought to leave," she says. "I was devastated. I was in my late twenties and had spent ten years of my life in the order. But in time I came to realize they were right. I had wanted to be a nun because I felt secure in the order, but I could never have been happy as a nun."

The feeling of rejection lingered for a couple of years as Barbara sought to find direction in her life. She moved to Denver to be near one of her sisters and took a personnel job at a bank. "I didn't want to return to teaching, but I didn't know quite what I wanted to do," she says.

WHAT'S THE CATCH?

Barbara underwent therapy for a time in Denver and then decided to drop out of the mainstream altogether. She lived off the small savings she had accumulated, became active in the feminist movement of the early 1970s, and tramped around in Europe for about a year. When she returned from Europe in 1973, she was flat broke and took a job in Denver with the investment firm she is with today.

"I had no intention of starting a career when I took the

job in Denver," she says. "I needed money for survival. I was
sleeping on two chairs because I didn't have any furniture
and was sometimes going hungry for three days." Barbara
liked her job, which was with a new service unit being
launched by the company, and threw all of her energies
into it, routinely working fifty to sixty hours a week to meet
or beat difficult deadlines. This time, her superiors re-
warded her. "They kept giving me more and more responsibility and more and more money, and I began to feel
accepted for the first time in my life," Barbara says. Her annual salary rose in a two-year period from $10,000 to
$50,000, which was more than Barbara had ever dreamed
of making.

Barbara was transferred to the company's New York
headquarters in 1975 and within five years was the highest-
paid woman on the company's payroll of 50,000-plus employees, with responsibility for a $25-million department
budget. She had a posh apartment in Manhattan and spent
the summers in a beach cottage on Long Island. It appeared that the poor girl from an alcoholic home in the
South had arrived at the age of forty-two. Inwardly, though,
she was confused.

"I was thinking, 'What do I do with all of this?' Part of
me was saying, 'I don't deserve this. What do people want
from me, or expect from me?' I never had trusted people's
motives, and I was puzzled about what I had done to get
where I was. I thought there was some catch to it."

Gambling had never been an option in Barbara Cummings' life until she moved to New York. She rarely had had
enough money to gamble, and gambling was certainly not a
big item in the convent, the hostels of Europe, or the radi-
cal feminist movement in which she was active.

In 1975, however, she was introduced to poker. One of
the managers with whom she worked asked her if she would
like to join several of the executives of the company for a

weekly poker game at one of the executives' apartments. She loved it immediately.

"It was a high-stakes game," she recalls, "and I thought it was exciting. You could win or lose four or five hundred dollars in a night. I could have played all night."

Barbara's skill and excitement were apparent to the other players. After she had played four or five times with the group, the man who had originally invited her to join the game pulled her aside and asked if she would consider withdrawing from the group. He said some of the men didn't feel comfortable playing with a woman.

"It really pissed me off," Barbara says, "but I went along because I worked with all these men and didn't want to jeopardize my working relationship with them. I think what they were really saying is that they didn't like to lose to a woman. After that, I forgot about poker for the next few years."

IGNORING THE WARNINGS

The next dramatic turn in Barbara's life came in 1980 when she left the company for an officer's position with another firm in the Los Angeles area. She realized quickly she had made a mistake in leaving and called her former boss to see if she could rejoin the company. Her old job had been filled, but she was offered a choice of three other jobs, one of which was a regional manager's post near where she was living. She decided to take it.

When Barbara decided to change jobs in 1980, she was not at a good point in her life. "I was emotionally distraught over a long affair I had with a married man in New York, and I wanted to get as far away from that situation as possible. I was in a period of emotional shutdown and wanted to meet new people and do new things."

Barbara soon discovered that the regional manager's job with her old company was boring in comparison with the high-powered posts she had held at corporate headquarters in New York. Fifty- to sixty-hour weeks were not required in her new job, so she began looking for outside interests. She soon found the outside interest she was searching for in the card clubs of Gardena, a few minutes from her home in the South Bay area of metropolitan Los Angeles.

"I had heard about the clubs from people who knew I liked to play poker," she says, "but I didn't go to check them out for about a year. The first time I went was the Friday after Thanksgiving in 1981. I watched people playing three-card draw at a three- to six-dollar table, and decided it looked like fun. So I joined in. I played four hours and won seventeen dollars. I had fun, and I thought the people were nice, but something in the back of my mind told me, 'This is trouble.'"

Barbara paid little heed to her inner warning. She returned to the card club the next night, the next, and every weekend for the next several months. She knew she was hooked ("it was something just waiting to happen"), but justified it by convincing herself that she was only going to the club to meet people and socialize.

Barbara also had $82,000 in the bank, so she reasoned that she could afford to play. "I thought, 'So what if I lose? It's my only hobby, and I know a lot of people who spend a thousand dollars a month on a hobby.'" Deep down, however, Barbara realized that her excursions to the card clubs were more than a hobby. Money wasn't important. She was hooked on the adrenaline rush she got from playing. "I would get this big rush, and I could go for hours without sleep," she says. "But when I got home after playing all weekend, I would go into this incredible depression. It was sort of a manic-depressive type existence."

For the first six months that she played, Barbara stuck with the three- to six-dollar-limit games and would usually win or lose $300 or $400 a weekend. She soon tired of that, however, and moved up to the five- to ten-dollar tables, and then to the ten-dollar-draw/$150-pot game, for which you paid $200 a night for a seat at the table.

TROUBLING SIGNALS EVERYWHERE

Within a year, the price tag of Barbara's hobby had risen dramatically. She had gone through half of her bankroll. To change her luck and break the monotony, she decided to switch card clubs. The switch only accelerated her losses. She picked a club that was frequented by professionals who feasted off compulsive gamblers.

She stepped up the action at the new club by playing the twenty- to forty-dollar and thirty- to sixty-dollar games. "It was high-stakes poker at its best," Barbara says. "If you weren't willing to risk a thousand dollars each time you played, then you had no business being there."

Barbara scored a number of big wins at the new venue. She won $13,000 during one weekend, and $8,000 and $7,000 at other times. She lost more than she won, however. "I lost thirteen thousand dollars in twenty-four hours once, and I was totally wiped out physically and mentally by the loss."

During this period, Barbara was also troubled by the failing health of a roommate named Sandy whom she had taken in to help defray rent expenses. Sandy was a female professional gambler Barbara had met at the club. A few months after Sandy moved in, she was diagnosed as having cancer. Barbara remembers feeling vaguely guilty about Sandy's cancer. "I don't know why," she says, "but somehow I felt like I was the cause of it."

Barbara quickly adopted a caretaker role with Sandy and was devastated when Sandy died in October 1984. "I was deeply depressed by her death," Barbara says. "I was angry with myself for hooking up with her in the first place, and I felt like I should have been able to do more to help her while she was dying. The way I coped was more gambling."

Shortly after Sandy's death, Barbara was $85,000 in debt. She had gone through her cash and had extended her credit cards to the limit as well as a $25,000 line of credit she had established. Most of her $75,000 salary was going to servicing debts and gambling. She also was passing bad checks and borrowing money from friends to make ends meet.

Barbara's health, which had always been robust, was now declining. She had a pronounced pallor, was unkempt, and suffered from total exhaustion. She was gambling every weekend from Friday afternoon to Sunday night at the club, stopping to rest for only a few minutes at a time in the women's room at the club. In an attempt to cover her losses and pay her bills, Barbara began to misuse her power at work by floating herself salary advances. It was a perilous practice, but it usually bought her some time.

LIFESAVING INSTINCTS

One weekend in 1985, everything came crashing down on Barbara. On Friday morning, she wrote herself a salary advance to cover checks she had written to pay off $3,000 in gambling losses, and went to the club that night intent on winning enough money to pay back her salary advance. She had to borrow $100 just to get in the game, but during the next eight hours, she won $8,000.

She thought, "Great, my problems are over," but she came back the next night and lost the $8,000, plus another $700. Barbara was devastated by the setback, but the next few minutes proved to be pivotal for her in what would be a long road to recovery from compulsive gambling. Driving home from the club, she was entertaining thoughts of suicide, when suddenly a big semi went out of control in front of her on the freeway and jackknifed. She reacted instinctively, swerving sharply to avoid a collision before lurching to a stop next to the outer freeway railing. "That seemed to snap me to my senses," Barbara says. "This big truck driver came running over to see if I was okay, and I told him, 'Yeah, I'm fine.' I drove the truck driver to a phone, and then I went home and went straight to bed. As I lay down I came to the realization that I needed help for my problem, and I made a decision to get the help the following morning. I slept well for the first time in weeks."

The next morning, Barbara called her boss in New York and told him her story. He told her not to worry and said he would talk to the Employee Assistance Department at the company and arrange for her to get some help. The Employee Assistance professional at the company called Barbara the next day and told her that he had arranged for her to enter a New England alcohol and drug treatment center that also treated compulsive gambling.

Barbara caught the next flight to New York, but found she had to wait two days for a room to open up at the center. She decided that while she was waiting she "might as well go out in flames." She drove to Atlantic City, where she won $7,000, which covered her share of the treatment costs and $4,000 in pressing debts.

She completed four weeks in treatment and received a new assignment with the company in New York so she could participate in a three-month, post-treatment, follow-up program, which included attending ninety GA or AA meetings in ninety days.

UNEASY TRUCE

Barbara didn't gamble during the period immediately following treatment, but she was hardly at peace with herself.

She missed the excitement of gambling and was filled with anger and resentment toward her employer. "I was pissed at having to take a demotion in New York, and I resented the hell out of the fact that they sent in a team of auditors to audit my old department in the Los Angeles office. I also found out that my boss's boss wanted to fire me."

Barbara didn't respond well to GA. "I thought it was a sexist group where the men told their war stories and nobody talked about feelings. I knew I had a problem, but I thought I could damn well do without those meetings. So I quit going to GA after the ninety days had passed." As would be expected, Barbara gradually began inching back into gambling. She knew she had a problem with playing poker, so she decided to switch games. She thought she might be able to control her gambling if she avoided poker.

Her first attempt at gambling was a qualified success. Barbara went to Atlantic City for the day, played the slots for three hours, and returned home even. Two months later, she tried it again, but ended up losing $400 or $500 on the slots.

Barbara felt somewhat guilty about gambling but still wasn't overly concerned, since she had contained her losses and hadn't felt that overpowering rush she had experienced at the poker parlors. Her illusion of control soon disappeared, however. Barbara was due to be transferred to a new job in Houston in the fall of 1986 and decided to take a trip to Los Angeles to visit her sister before she moved. The trip turned into a disaster. Barbara never made it to her sister's house from the airport. Against her better judgment, she stopped by the card club in Gardena to play a few hands of poker for old time's sake. She used her company-issued credit card to obtain a $1,500 cash advance, and within a few hours, she had lost $1,200. She was able to quit before she lost the full amount, but unbeknownst to her, her troubles had now begun in earnest.

The cash advance Barbara had drawn at the club had put her over the limit on her company credit card, and her account was "red flagged" at corporate headquarters in New York and forwarded to Barbara's boss. He examined Barbara's account and noticed that Barbara had used the credit card at the club in Gardena. He also spotted a cash advance at a casino in Atlantic City a few weeks earlier.

"He was ripped," Barbara says, "and he confronted me immediately. He placed me on a two-week suspension while he met with the Employee Assistance people, personnel, and company lawyers. Even though I was in limbo for two weeks, it was a moment of truth for me. I knew I had to quit gambling. It was that or oblivion. But I honestly didn't know if I could quit. It was frightening." Barbara received another chance. She was referred by the company to the Taylor Manor compulsive gambling treatment program in Ellicott City, Maryland.

ANOTHER TRY

Barbara was relieved that the company hadn't fired her, but she was apprehensive about entering another treatment program. Her anxiety peaked as she was driving south through New Jersey on her way from New York to Maryland. "I actually thought about stopping in Atlantic City on the way to Maryland," Barbara says. "I thought nobody will know. I got lucky, though. I somehow missed the Atlantic City exit and was ten miles past it before I realized it. So I just kept going."

When she arrived at Taylor Manor, Barbara wished she had stopped in Atlantic City. "It never occurred to me that Taylor Manor was a psychiatric hospital," she says. "I thought it would be more like the alcohol and drug treatment center in New England. When I was admitted, they treated me like a crazy person. They took my possessions away and put me in a locked unit. I was angry and uncooperative for two weeks and wouldn't talk to anyone. But when I left after seven weeks, I felt much differently. I began facing the issues in my life for the first time and left feeling that I could do anything in life except gamble."

Barbara Cummings hasn't gambled since, and in 1989 she paid the last installment on the huge debt she ran up during her gambling days.

Barbara Cummings is an intelligent, insightful woman, who has changed her life dramatically by painstakingly sorting through the bitter memories of her childhood and her self-destructive behavior. She says she learned three important things about herself during her seven weeks of treatment at Taylor Manor. She came to understand that she had been depressed for fifteen years and didn't know it. She learned to be more accepting of who she was and to be more comfortable with herself. And she learned to rid herself of her martyr, or savior, complex.

"I know I am going to continue to have thoughts about gambling—that's not going to disappear like magic—but I don't have to give in to those thoughts because I don't need to escape any longer. There are other ways for me to deal with my fears and anxieties.

"There are large parts of me that are healthy, and parts of me that are unhealthy, but I don't have to overcompensate any longer for the parts of me that are unhealthy. It has been a very freeing experience for me to realize that I don't have to be perfect to earn approval or respect. I feel strong now, and feel good about myself."

Barbara says she still is working through some anger about the past, but feels that she is making progress. She knows from experience that she will have to be on guard against a relapse, but adds that she doesn't dwell on the possibility. "Today, I'm not afraid to ask for help. Before, when I relapsed, I had to be coerced into getting help. I feel fortunate that is all behind me now."

THE MONTEREY **1 3**

MEETING:

ONE DAY AT A TIME

When Mike Brubaker moved to the Monterey, California, area from Los Angeles in 1988, one of the first things he noticed was that there was no self-help meeting for compulsive gamblers on the Monterey Peninsula or in the immediate area.

Upon investigation, he discovered that there had been a meeting in Monterey a few years earlier, but it had disbanded when its founder, a man named Larry, resumed gambling. The nearest help was a small Tuesday night meeting in a private home in Aptos, a city of about 9,000 people 40 miles north of Monterey. The only other meetings within a reasonable distance were in San Jose, more than an hour's drive away.

"I thought we needed at least one meeting in an area of over 300,000 people," he says. "It's difficult enough to get gamblers to attend a meeting next door, much less an hour away."

Mike also wanted a meeting for himself. As part of his ongoing recovery, he attends a minimum of three self-help meetings a week for alcoholism and compulsive gambling. Therefore, almost as soon as he touched foot in Monterey,

Mike set about organizing a meeting. He located Larry, the prodigal gambler who had started the Monterey meeting that folded, to enlist his support, put out feelers at the Aptos and San Jose meetings for compulsive gamblers in the Monterey area, and began collecting names of people making inquiries about gambling problems at Community Hospital Recovery Center where he now worked.

By February 1989, he had rounded up enough people for an inaugural meeting, which took place on a Thursday night in a modular building called the Education Annex on the back lot of Community Hospital Recovery Center. Five people attended that meeting, including Mike and Larry. Now more than a year later, the Thursday night compulsive gamblers meeting has become a fixture in Monterey.

As a cool breeze blew in from Monterey Bay on a spring night in 1990, Mike Brubaker arrived a few minutes earlier than usual for the Thursday compulsive gamblers meeting. There had been another meeting in the Education Annex earlier in the evening and Mike felt he needed extra time to "check out the meeting room and the coffee situation."

Mike had been looking forward to the meeting throughout the day. He was anticipating a good turnout. Three new people had told him they were coming—two current patients in the alcohol and drug program at Community Hospital Recovery Center and an attractive, young woman whom Mike had known for several years. The woman, a recovering alcoholic, was currently on the fence about whether she had a gambling problem. Mike, who usually sees things as black or white, felt certain that she did.

Mike had left the hospital three hours earlier after a rather hectic day in which both he and his boss, Len Baltzer, had dealt with crises precipitated by relapses of former patients. He had rushed home for a small dinner party he and his wife, Donna, were giving for a friend who was celebrating his seventh year of sobriety in Alcoholics Anonymous, and had exchanged his coat and tie for a white jogging suit before heading back to the hospital for the meeting. Three people from the Thursday night compulsive gamblers group also attended the dinner party at the Brubakers', including Alex Petros, who lived around the corner and up the hill from Mike and Donna.

THE GROUP GATHERS

A few pleasant surprises were in store for Mike at the Thursday-night meeting. Instead of the usual turnout of seven or eight, thirteen people showed up, including two people Mike hadn't expected. A third patient from the alcohol and drug treatment program was there, as well as Vinnie Maggio, the restaurant manager Mike Brubaker had confronted about his compulsive gambling problem when he was in treatment for alcoholism the previous fall at Community Hospital Recovery Center.

Vinnie had taken a night manager's job at an all-night restaurant in Monterey a couple of months earlier and hadn't attended the Thursday night meeting in more than a month. Moreover, he had fallen out of touch with Mike and others in the group, which is often an ominous sign. Mike was to discover that Vinnie had indeed gone on an alcohol bender only three days earlier, but Vinnie insisted that he had refrained from gambling since last October. Mike, who wasn't sure that Vinnie was being honest about his gambling, was very pleased about Vinnie's return to the group. He regarded it as a good sign.

The other bit of good news Mike was to receive on Thursday night was that some members of the group wanted to start a second meeting in Monterey. Mike told the group that he would be unable to make the same commitment to a second meeting that he had made to the first, but that he would help in any way he could to get another meeting off the ground.

"A second meeting would be great," Mike said afterward, "but someone other than me has to share in the commitment to get it started. Organizing and running meetings is a key part of the Twelve Step service philosophy. I hope somebody in the group will step forward and take responsibility for a new meeting. I'll guarantee you that the person who does step forward will have a better chance of not gambling than someone who only attends a meeting once a week."

The meeting on this Thursday night was basically an exchange of stories. Everyone participated with the exception of the young woman who was attending at Mike Brubaker's urging. She declined to identify herself as a compulsive gambler and seemed somewhat exasperated with Mike at the beginning of the meeting when he asked her to read the traditions of the group. She rolled her eyes and with a trace of sarcasm, said, "Sure, Michael. Anything you say."

Among those gathered at a single table in the long meeting room were two men with ten or more years of recovery from alcohol and drugs. One was a muscular government worker wearing an "Easy Does It" T-shirt symbolic of his membership in AA, and the other was a former tennis professional who drove over from San Jose with another gambler, a tall young computer specialist. The man in the T-shirt had gone on a gambling binge in Tahoe a few days earlier. The tennis pro was marking his eighty-sixth consecutive day without gambling. The computer specialist was coming off a big gambling spree that had ended, at least temporarily, forty-eight hours earlier. The computer specialist said he was uncertain what tomorrow would bring.

Mike Brubaker, with eleven-plus years of recovery, was the only person in the room with more than a year of full-fledged recovery from compulsive gambling. Another member of the group, Bill Williams, hadn't made a bet since 1984, but he had engaged in profligate borrowing less than a year earlier, which had forced him into bank-ruptcy and placed him in jeopardy of having his probation revoked for a gambling-related felony. Bill's wife, Marie, who had suffered tremendously under the weight of her husband's gambling, was also at the meeting. Both she and Bill had been regulars at the meeting since the formation of the group thirteen months earlier.

The only others at the meeting were two regulars, a ruggedly handsome doctor in a red windbreaker with nine months of recovery, whom Mike had targeted as a good candidate to lead a second meeting, and Alex Petros, the one-time bon vivant who had won and lost great sums at the casinos of Lake Tahoe and the card parlors around San Francisco.

Alex had not laid down a bet since September 10, 1989, when he lost more than $100,000 in a pia gow game at a card club near San Francisco International Airport.

Mike Brubaker had been concerned about Alex Petros' recovery when Alex and his girlfriend, Julie, had winged off to England for an extended vacation a couple of months into his recovery. Mike had recommended to Alex that he attend Gamblers Anonymous meetings while he was in England, and Alex had done so.

The meetings Alex attended in London were large gatherings of more than a hundred people each. Alex was left with the impression that compulsive gambling is even a bigger problem in England than it is in the United States, but he adds ruefully that he thinks we'll catch up as gambling becomes more accessible in this country.

"Gambling is everywhere in England," he says. "There's an off-track-betting booth on every corner in London, as well as casinos for the wealthy, slot machines, lotteries, and the like. I got the feeling that everybody in London gambled. I had never noticed all the betting when I was there before, but I did this time."

R E S I S T I N G   T E M P T A T I O N

Alex believes his recovery from gambling would not be so difficult if there were no gambling in California. From time to time in his recovery, he has experienced what he describes as flashes, or impulses, to gamble. He feels infinitely more secure when he's out of harm's way and the San Francisco card parlors.

"When I'm in San Francisco, I'm never more than a few minutes away from a card club," he says, "and, quite frankly, I don't want to be there when one of those flashes comes over me. I feel that if I have to go through the process of catching a plane or driving to Tahoe [three hours away by car], I'll have time to come to my senses before I start gambling."

In an effort to cope with this fear, Alex spends much of his time at his weekend home in Carmel, which is a two-hour drive from his primary residence in San Francisco. To ensure this, he has committed himself to three recovery-oriented meetings a week in the Carmel area. He attends the self-help meeting on Thursday night, attends an aftercare meeting for former patients at Community Hospital Recovery Center on Friday morning, and has a one-hour session with his psychiatrist in Carmel every Friday afternoon.

Alex says he doesn't always like the self-help meetings, but he believes the meetings are essential to his recovery. "I know I can't just do things I like," he says. "That's what I used to do, and it got me into trouble." He believes it is important for him to make commitments and stick to them. In the past, he never concerned himself about commitments. Alex's psychiatrist, who's a stern, seventy-five-year-old father figure, has told Alex that he will not tolerate his missing or being late for an appointment. Alex is required to give the psychiatrist three weeks' notice if he's planning to miss an appointment, as well as the reason why. "I won't miss an appointment with him no matter what," Alex says with a laugh. "I don't want to get him upset."

Because he's still relatively wealthy despite gambling losses of $3 million to $5 million in a two-year period, Alex says he has some difficulty relating to others in GA, and vice versa. "Most of the people in GA have been financially devastated," Alex says, "and at times, I feel that some of them don't relate to my story because I haven't been totally wiped out. But I think recovery is just as difficult for a wealthy person as it is for anyone else. I was accustomed to living on $500,000 or $600,000 a year, and doing anything I wanted to do. Now, I am out of cash, and trying to live within my income from real estate investments. It's been a big adjustment for me, and one that I find difficult at times."

The owner of one of the San Francisco card clubs where Alex played pia gow pulled Alex aside one night during the midst of a big spree and told him he'd better slow down. "He told me that most people who lose everything could adjust to living in a one-room apartment, but he didn't think I could. He told me I ought to stop gambling for my own sake before it was too late."

Alex still owes the club owner $50,000 and has promised to pay him back gradually. "I could sell some assets and pay it back all at once," Alex says, "but I don't want to. I need to be reminded that I owe money because of my gambling."

Alex believes that he can no more afford one more gambling binge than anyone else in GA. "If I do gamble again, I'll lose everything I have and be disinherited by my mother. I don't think I'm strong enough to survive that. I believe I would take a jump or kill myself some other way. It would be oblivion for me."

HIGH PRICE OF BOREDOM

Alex could embellish his current standard of living by selling assets, but he has decided against that. "I don't want the temptation of having a couple of million dollars in cash laying around. I don't want to sell anything until I am ready to invest it in a business or something else worthwhile." For the present, Alex is concentrating on slowing down his once-frenetic life-style and proceeding with great caution in making decisions that could affect the rest of his life. Even though he is looking forward to starting a business or finding a job, he wants to avoid making a rash decision. He has set a timeframe of six more months before making a decision about a career, which would coincide roughly with the first anniversary of the date he stopped gambling.

"I don't want to set myself up for disappointment or failure in business," Alex says. "I need to think things through clearly and be successful in whatever I ultimately decide to do."

Alex plans each day carefully. He usually rises at six o'clock and follows a tight schedule that allows for no idle time. He allots time to gardening, tending to business affairs, reading, and a round of golf, if time permits. He usually retires about 8:30 or 9:00. "I've never had structure in my life," Alex says, "so adhering to a schedule is very important for me. I can't afford idle time or boredom. I know a relapse can happen and I know it's more likely to occur if I'm bored or have too much time on my hands. A relapse is always on my mind and I'm very cautious."

Despite all the precautions he's taking, Alex realizes that he's extremely vulnerable. This point was driven home during the first two weeks of March, when Alex entered a guilt-induced depression over a serious family squabble that culminated in his mother removing his brother Tony from her will.

Even though the split between his mother and brother occurred over a dispute concerning Tony's eight-year-old son, Alex felt responsible because the relationship between the two had been strained ever since Alex entered treatment for compulsive gambling and drug dependency five months earlier.

Alex says his mother thought Tony should have been

more supportive of him while he was in treatment. She had been cool and distant to Tony in the months following Alex's discharge. On the other hand, Alex says, Tony resented the fact that his mother paid for his treatment and was overly protective of him. Tony shouted to his mother during a rage, "What did I do to be disinherited? Every time Alex is in trouble, I'm the one who gets blamed."

"Regardless of who was right, I blamed myself," Alex says, "and I felt even worse because I was the one who would benefit from Tony's disinheritance. I became very depressed, and didn't see how I was going to get through it. What helped turn me around was when my psychiatrist pointed out to me that my mother's and Tony's relationship had been strained long before I started gambling and that I wasn't the cause of the difficulty between them.

"I have come to realize that I'm not the cause of family problems. In fact, it's just the opposite. One of the causes of my problems is that I come from a very dysfunctional family in which I was not allowed to grow up. I was never able to see life as it really was."

On the morning following the Thursday-night compulsive gamblers' meeting in Monterey, Alex Petros sat in his favorite breakfast spot in Carmel, enjoying bacon and eggs, sipping coffee, and chain-smoking cigarettes as he discussed the insights he has gained into his behavior since he stopped gambling.

Alex, an engaging man, carried on a lively banter with the waitress and restaurant owner at intervals during the discussion. As a former restaurant owner, Alex is comfortable with restaurant people and is picky about where he eats. He calls the small cafe off the main drag of Carmel "absolutely the best breakfast place in Carmel" and eats there almost every day he's in town.

As he dissected his innermost feelings about recovery, Alex occasionally groped for words, but he carried on until he found the right words to describe how he felt. Although he had only reluctantly agreed to discuss his gambling a few months earlier, Alex now seemed eager to share his thoughts and feelings.

SUCCUMBING TO A FEAR OF FAILURE

He talked about how his adopted father, a self-made millionaire, was put on a pedestal after he died while Alex was very young and how he felt as if he never measured up to his father and what was expected of him. "I wanted to be like my father," he says, "and felt like great things were expected of me. But my little failures became big to me, and I felt like I had let everyone down."

Alex says he gradually developed a fear of failure, which led to his being overly cautious in everything he did. He also began to procrastinate. "I began to sit on the sidelines and let everything pass me by," he says. "On the one hand I had no self-esteem whatsoever, but on the other, I felt I was very special and that I had a very special purpose in life."

Alex found early in life that he enjoyed the thrill and competition of gambling. When he was in his teens he would risk his mother's disapproval to slip into a back room to play poker with his uncles, all of whom worked for his mother in the family business. "I remember she would get mad at my uncles, and scold them for taking advantage of me," Alex says. "The truth of the matter was that I was the one at fault. I would pester my uncles until they let me play with them."

Alex continued to gamble. It made him feel powerful and in control, even when he lost. Once when he was twenty-one, he lost $4,000 playing dice in a rigged game at a bar. He said he shouldn't have covered his losses because the game was rigged, but he returned the next day to pay off the full amount. "I had this idea that honor was an important part of gambling. You went into it with your eyes wide open, and you paid up when you lost. It was the manly, honorable thing to do."

Alex never really lost more than he could afford until years later, in 1987, when it became obvious that he could no longer control his impulse to gamble. As his losses mounted, he became wracked with guilt about the money he was wasting.

"I had done some work with the homeless through my church in San Francisco," Alex says, "and I thought how much I could have helped if I had given the $4 million I had lost gambling to the church. I felt like I had committed a mortal sin. I had always craved money and power, but when I lost, I felt greedy and stupid and sinful. I couldn't justify my actions to myself any longer, and I was deeply depressed, even when I won."

Alex says he realizes today that he gambled because he was mentally ill. He says that realization has helped him deal with his guilt. He's working the steps of the GA program and says one of the most cleansing steps for him thus far "was making amends to the people I've hurt. I used to think the only person I was hurting was myself, but I was only deluding myself."

Since he quit gambling, Alex says he's now communicating better with people, including his mother and his girlfriend, Julie. He is trying to convince Julie to attend Gam-Anon. "I tell her she ought to go so she can learn how to be a real bitch," he says with a laugh.

Alex says the issue with which he continues to have the most difficulty in his recovery is his sense that he is somehow different from other people. "I've learned some humility in my recovery," he says, "but the feeling that I'm in some way special or different continues to haunt me. I sometimes think I was destined to be a conquering hero or something on that order. I've lain awake at night trying to work through it, but without a lot of success. I'm very aware it's not a healthy feeling."

• • •

FITTING THE PIECES TOGETHER

Alex, who turned forty in March 1990, is struggling to force himself to look ahead instead of backward. "When I turned forty, my first impulse was to look at my life as a total failure," he says, "but I've got a chance to do better in my next twenty years than in my last twenty. At times I have trouble focusing on the future instead of the past, but I think I can turn my thinking around if I follow the one-day-at-a-time philosophy."

Dreams about gambling are another major source of anxiety for Alex. His dreams about relapsing occur as often as twice a week. Although he doesn't recall the content of his dreams in any great detail, he is aware that he becomes depressed in his dream after succumbing to the compulsion to gamble.

"The dreams are nightmares, really," Alex says. "I'm always struggling with myself in my dreams and always end up gambling. I wake up in a state of panic and am relieved to discover I was only dreaming. But the feeling of depression from the dream usually carries over for a couple of hours after I get up in the morning. The dreams are very vivid and very real. Hopefully, they will subside in time. I've started keeping a pad by my bed to write down the contents of the dreams as they occur so the psychiatrist can help me with them."

Despite the dreams and the other difficulties facing him in recovery, Alex Petros reports that he feels much stronger than he did when he was discharged from Community Hospital Recovery Center, and his strength continues to grow. "I'm going to keep going to my meetings and seeing the psychiatrist until the pieces start falling into place for me," he says.

After breakfast, Alex hopped in his car for a drive to Monterey for his aftercare meeting at the hospital. As he pulled away from the curb, he checked the clock in his car, which read eight twenty A.M., and said with a grin, "I guess I had better hurry, or I'm going to be late for my eight thirty aftercare meeting. I'm not supposed to be late for appointments, you know."

MONEY GAMES

After Marie Williams had talked briefly at the Thursday compulsive gamblers meeting in Monterey, the broad-shouldered man in the "Easy Does It" T-shirt looked across the table at the fifty-seven-year-old mother of three and said: "Marie, I'm so glad you're here. Your smile always brings so much to this meeting."

Marie smiled graciously and averted her eyes slightly. Her eyes were moist. Although Marie is not a compulsive gambler, the Thursday-night meeting has been a godsend to her. Four months before the start-up of the meeting, Marie was devastated by the latest in a series of shocks that turned her once secure Midwestern existence into a nightmare.

In October 1988, as Marie was tending to her flowers in front of her home in Carmel, a young man whom she knew pulled up in a car, hurried over to her, and asked in an excited tone of voice whether Bill was home.

After Marie had told the man Bill wasn't home, he blurted out rather sharply: "Marie, tell him I've got to see him. Now. He owes me a lot of money."

Marie reacted to his words as though she had been shot. She thought: "Oh no, Bill's gambling again."

She recalled later, "As I stood there in the yard, I didn't know what to do or how to feel. It was as if the very life was draining out of me."

As it turned out, Bill had not been gambling—not in the strictest sense of the word. But he had been borrowing heavily from friends, and in October 1988, the string had begun to run out for him.

Bill had been borrowing and juggling money for the last four years, and he owed fourteen people a total of $110,000, with no possible means of repaying it. He says the reason he borrowed was to keep up appearances. "I was borrowing to look good to other people," Bill says. "I remember one time I was with a group of guys at a bar in Monterey, and a couple of them put up two hundred dollars for some kind of charity. I was worried how I was going to pay the rent, but I put up two hundred dollars anyway, just to look good. Inwardly, I felt terrible. I had no peace of mind. But it was important for me to look good to others."

A LITTLE BIT AT A TIME

To Marie, the borrowing and the offhand way she found out about it was painfully reminiscent of a time eight years earlier, when she first discovered that Bill had gambled away everything she had held dear. On that October day in 1988, Marie told her daughter that she may have overcome the first disaster in Indianapolis, but this time, she believed her life was over. Marie didn't think she had the strength or courage to rebuild her life again.

Marie, however, found the strength once again. She heard about an upcoming gambling presentation in Mon-

terey and prevailed upon Bill to attend with her. The pre-
senter was Mike Brubaker. Following the presentation, Bill
and Marie met privately with Mike who told them about his
plans to start up a compulsive gamblers meeting. Marie ea-
gerly embraced the idea of a meeting. Bill was noticeably
less eager.

Mike recalls his private meeting with Marie and Bill in
some detail. He says Marie was very upset and did virtually
all the talking, while Bill sat quietly with a downcast expression. Mike suspected correctly that Bill had not revealed the
full details of his borrowing to Marie. In the days and weeks
ahead, Bill gradually came clean about the extent of his borrowing and about another brief fling with gambling in 1984.
"I don't know why," Bill said, "but I never could bring myself
to tell Marie or the kids everything at once. I just told them
what I wanted them to hear, a little bit at a time. I was the
very same way when I was a kid. I lied every time my mother
and my father confronted me about something."

By March 1989, Bill had no choice but to divulge the size
of his debts. For the second time in eight years, he was
forced into bankruptcy. Unlike the first time, when he simply walked away from $750,000 in debts to a group of
friends in Indianapolis, Bill agreed to make restitution
over a four-year period on a sliding rate that began at
$1,000 a month and accelerated to $2,100 a month after a
year. "It's very difficult at times to make the payments, but I
would rather live this way than the way we were before,"
says Marie, who works as an interior decorator and "Girl
Friday" for a well-to-do widow in the area.

As of March 1990, however, the Williamses' problems
were far from over.

As he talked in March 1990 about his history of compulsive
gambling and reckless borrowing, Bill Williams was facing
the threat of being returned to federal court in New Jersey
for violation of the terms of a five-year probated sentence
for mail fraud.

Bill had lived on the edge continuously for much of his adult life, but it was nothing like this. "I'm in danger of having my probation revoked from now until July," he said. "I'm sweating it out until then. The stress has been terrible."

The threat to Bill Williams' probation arose from a criminal charge filed by one of his creditors in the Monterey area. The creditor was not satisfied by the bankruptcy and restitution plan approved by the court, claiming that Bill had borrowed money from him with the intent to defraud.

"Most of the people I borrowed money from here were supportive of the restitution plan," Bill said. "Three or four of them even called to wish me luck in turning my life around. But this one guy arrived at the house one day and almost beat the door in trying to get at me. He filed criminal charges despite attempts by my attorney and some other people to cool him down. If I have to go to prison, he's not going to get his money back, but I think he's more interested in revenge. I'm not sure I can blame him."

TURNING STRESS INTO PEACE

Bill admits that he borrowed money under false pretenses and says he is now undergoing psychological counseling to try to get at the underlying causes of his problems. "For the first time in my life," he says, "I'm willing to do what's necessary to turn things around."

The stress under which Bill and Marie have been living has had an apparent effect on their health. Marie underwent surgery for breast cancer in April 1987, and about a month before he was to appear in a bankruptcy court in Monterey, Bill underwent surgery for the removal of a brain tumor in his left temporal area. Bill's doctors ventured an opinion that his tumor could have been caused by stress. Though their recovery has gone well, the expense of the two operations added significantly to their financial burdens.

"At times, I have wondered just how much more I could take," Marie says, "but I guess I'm a much stronger person than I could ever have imagined. Other people have told me they always knew I was a strong person, but I had always thought I was a very weak person. I am trying to take things one day at a time, and so far it's working for me, and for us."

Bill Williams says that despite the threat of possible court action, he is happy for the first time in years. He enjoys working with his hands in his painting and carpentry business and is much more at peace with himself. "I plan to make the most of this chance," he says. "I didn't enjoy the compulsive gamblers meetings at first, but I think they are helping me now. My biggest regret is that I didn't take advantage of my second chance when I had it [in 1980, after the Indianapolis bankruptcy], but this time, I'm doing things differently. This is my last chance. I want to change for my sake and Marie's sake."

Bill Williams would seem to be an unlikely candidate for a compulsive gambler. He is a quiet, soft-spoken, youthful-looking, fifty-nine-year-old man with a pleasant, unassuming manner.

Bill, however, has always lived two lives—one as an industrious, loving father and husband, and the other as an extraordinary risk taker and high roller. The only time the two worlds merged for the public to see was in the late 1970s, when Bill began racing expensive high-performance cars on the Atlantic Coast at the age of forty-seven. He says he received the same excitement from racing as he did from gambling but felt better about it since it was a pursuit he could share with his family and friends. Racing Porsches, however, was almost as expensive a hobby as gambling— $2,000 a weekend—and it was putting an enormous strain on the already strained finances of the Williams family.

A Very Convincing Liar

Two years later Bill Williams' secret life finally became public, much to the shock of Marie and hundreds of other people in the tight-knit section of Indianapolis where they lived. In an instant, everything they had was gone—the race cars, two homes, a twenty-seven-acre farm, Bill's thriving insurance business, Marie's gourmet cooking store, and their friends. The worst cut of all, however, was an indictment returned against Bill in New Jersey for mail fraud. He had used a $46,000 insurance premium from a business customer to pay off some debts and had failed to cover the premium before it was due at the headquarters of the insurance company in New Jersey. The case would drag on in Federal court for almost four years before Bill would receive a five-year probated sentence and a stiff fine from the court.

Bill had lost approximately $3 million gambling in a twelve-year period spanning from 1968 to 1980. The most incredible part of his story, however, was the fact that he had managed to keep his gambling and heavy losses a secret from Marie, his three children, and many of his closest friends and associates.

"Two of my children said, 'Mother, how could you have not known?' " Marie says, "and I've asked myself the same question a million times. I knew Bill liked to gamble, but I never suspected anything like what happened. Looking back now, it's easy to see the signs—the telephone calls from people I didn't know and Bill's evasiveness about some things. But back then, I didn't have any reason to doubt Bill. He'd always been a good husband and father, and we loved one another. I hate to say it, but Bill was a very convincing liar."

Bill Williams began gambling at an early age, but managed to keep it a secret from his parents. He was a hard-working youth, who had a paper route and worked at a grocery store. For recreation, he played nickel-and-dime poker and bet on sporting events and horse races. He supplemented his income by selling betting cards and playing slot machines with dime and quarter slugs that he and some of his friends had made by melting down toy soldiers. Much to his surprise, the FBI came to his neighborhood when he was in the seventh grade to investigate the source of the slugs. When he learned of the investigation at the grocery store where he worked, he hurried home and got rid of a coffee can full of slugs he had in his room.

He was never close to his parents or his brothers when he was growing up, and he was anxious to leave home for college in the early 1950s. Bill and Marie began dating while they were in high school and were married during Bill's freshman year at a large midwestern university. He was nineteen and she was seventeen.

For the next fifteen years Bill quit gambling altogether as he threw all of his energies into finishing college, raising a family, and launching a life and pension insurance business in Indianapolis. Bill put in long hours in his business, prospecting for new clients and servicing existing ones. After about a dozen years, Bill's firm was one of the most prosperous insurance agencies in Indianapolis.

"Once you establish an insurance business you can live very comfortably off repeat sales," Bill says. "I had worked hard and had done better than I had expected so I decided to enjoy myself for a while. I also had plenty of money for the first time in my life—which had been my goal in starting the business."

Bill whiled away his idle time playing golf and poker at the country club to which he belonged. He played poker at the club every Wednesday night for a period of about two years before losing interest in the quarter to two-dollar games, with five- to ten-dollar pots. "It just wasn't exciting enough," Bill says. "I started looking for high-stakes games and a lot of action. Most of the time I didn't care if I won or lost; I just wanted to be in the game."

Raising the Stakes

Bill soon plugged into a network of high-stakes poker games in hotel rooms around Indianapolis, which were operated by organized crime syndicates from Chicago, Cleveland, and Detroit. The games more than satisfied Bill's quest for excitement. The pots were usually in the $1,500 to $2,000 range, and accordingly the game itself was filled with tension and a suggestion of danger.

"Everything was on a first-name-only basis," Bill says. "I never once played with anyone I knew. I suspected that a lot of the players were mob connected, but that didn't bother me. I could win four thousand to five thousand dollars in a couple of hours, or lose it just as fast. I was a good player until I got way ahead, but then I did dumb things."

Once Bill gave another player a bad check for $5,000 and received a threatening phone call the next day. He says a menacing black car followed him everywhere he went and parked outside of his house at night until he made good on the check a couple of days later. "I learned then that those guys really meant business," he says, "so I never tried that trick again."

Sometimes Bill would hear about a big game out of town and would leave town for a couple of days on a fake business trip to participate in the game. Generally, though, he confined his playing to weekdays to keep his gambling hidden from Marie and the family. He was home almost every night and made it a rule to never play on weekends. "That eased my conscience, too," he says. "I could justify playing to myself because I never let it interfere with my family life."

Although he won frequently, Bill soon began accumulating heavy debts from his gambling losses. "Those games in the hotel rooms were almost like playing against the house," he says. "If you played long enough and didn't know when to quit, like me, you were going to end up losing. I always bet more than I intended to and played longer than I should have just to stay in the game. I felt like I had power and control when I was playing poker. I never felt that way in any other type of gambling."

To cover his losses, Bill took out three mortgages on his properties and began borrowing money from friends and business associates. He never told his friends the real reason he needed the money. He would fabricate stories concerning his business or failed investments. "I always paid my friends back as quickly as possible even if it meant having to borrow from another friend," Bill says. "That way I knew they would be good for more money if I needed it."

Although he was on an insane course and was constantly juggling loans and under intense pressure, Bill says borrowing gave him almost as big a rush as gambling. "I would lie awake at night plotting how to get money the next day," he says. "It was stressful, but it was exciting. I never considered cutting back on our life-style because I liked having a big home and fast cars. I liked all that. It made me feel important."

Because of high interest rates and continued gambling losses, Bill's obligations grew almost daily. To buy a little time, he began skimming his customers' insurance premiums, which were made out to his firm and then forwarded to New Jersey minus his commission. The plan worked for a period of time, but when Bill was late covering the $46,000 premium paid by one of his customers, he was summoned immediately to New Jersey.

HOUSE OF CARDS COLLAPSES

Bill thought he might be able to pacify the insurance company, but his hopes were soon dashed. The company told him it was revoking his license and was considering criminal charges. The notice that his license had been revoked was waiting for Bill at his office when he returned to Indianapolis.

"I knew it was all over," Bill says, "and I was totally defeated and humiliated. I knew I had to tell Marie and the kids, but I really didn't know how to go about it. I knew I would never be able to face my friends again or even talk to them."

On the weekend after he had returned from New Jersey, Bill called a family meeting around the kitchen table in their home in an exclusive area of Indianapolis. All Bill had revealed to Marie up to that point was that he was sick and really wasn't feeling well, but now he began recounting in bits and pieces what had happened. He said he had borrowed a lot of money, which he was unable to repay, and that he was going to lose his business. He also said he had lost a lot of money gambling.

Marie reacted at first with disbelief and then anger. Bill remembers that Marie seemed "disgusted" with him and that eventually she began to cry, as did their daughter. Bill and Marie's two sons reacted mostly with disbelief, but pledged to support their father.

Bill stopped far short of telling the full story. In fact, Marie says she didn't learn all the details of their financial affairs until she and Bill met with an attorney a few days later. "I was flabbergasted at the lawyer's office when Bill laid everything out," Marie says. "I had no idea things were as bad as they were. Up until then, I thought there may be some hope. I was really angry with Bill for not telling me everything, but he was so depressed and suicidal that I swallowed my anger."

The Williamses declared bankruptcy and in the days and weeks that followed Marie's life was a nightmare. Once, she came home to find herself barred from her house by a team of workers who were "red-tagging" cars, furniture and other belongings for auction. "That was the last straw for me," she says. "I began shouting and screaming, and called our attorney who finally got the people out of my house."

What stung Marie even more was the way she was shunned by her friends and neighbors. She says people would stare at her in the grocery store and go out of their way to avoid speaking to her. Marie sought solace from her parish priest but he also rebuffed her, saying that Bill had sinned.

"Even though we had lived in Indianapolis our whole lives, I knew I couldn't stay there any longer," Marie says. "I told Bill he could stay if he wanted, but I was leaving. We finally moved in 1982, about a year after everything had fallen apart for us."

One of Bill and Marie's two sons still lives in Indianapolis, as does Marie's father and Bill's mother. Bill and Marie have been back to Indianapolis only once since they left. While he was there, Bill tried to set up lunch with one of his old friends from whom he had borrowed money. Bill says his friend was cordial over the phone, but was unable to meet him for lunch. Not long after that, Bill's friend died suddenly.

"It was a sad moment for me when I learned he had died," Bill says. "We had been friends since childhood, and I wanted to see him face to face one more time to tell him how sorry I was for what had happened."

Bill and Marie originally planned to settle in Los Angeles where Bill had a job offer, but they didn't like L.A. They moved farther north to Carmel to be closer to their daughter and her family.

On their way from Indianapolis to Los Angeles, however, Bill persuaded Marie to stop in Las Vegas where he tried his luck at blackjack. This little stop was a portent of what was to come. Despite their problems back home, Marie still didn't understand the nature of compulsive gambling, and neither did Bill.

Bill Williams found work in Carmel but the couple's lifestyle was a far cry from what it had been in Indiana. For a period of a few weeks they ate their meals off cardboard boxes in their rented apartment.

Bill felt depressed. The court case in New Jersey was hanging over his head, and he was unable to find relief from the tremendous guilt he felt over wrecking his and Marie's life. "There was so much uncertainty," he says. "I was worried about going to prison and I didn't know what I wanted to do. All I knew was insurance and I couldn't do that any longer because my license had been pulled." Bill dealt with his depression the only way he knew how. He began playing poker again. This time he played on a small scale for a couple of years with a group of friends. Playing poker made Bill feel better, but eventually, it began to frustrate him because he couldn't afford to play for high stakes. He simply wasn't getting the rush from gambling that he had experienced before.

"I tried to justify playing poker in my own mind," Bill says, "but I never really could. I felt guilty and poor. I was just playing to win a few bucks. The excitement was missing. If I had had some money I think it would have been different. I probably would have gone off the deep end again."

A DIFFERENT TYPE OF RISK

Bill quit playing poker when his five-year probated sentence was handed down in New Jersey. He was assigned to a probation officer to whom he had to report periodically. Things didn't improve dramatically for the Williamses in the two years that followed, so in 1986 Bill decided to take a different type of risk. He applied for a California insurance license and lied on the question which asked if he had ever been convicted of a felony. The license was granted and Bill set up shop in Carmel.

"I hoped they wouldn't check on the felony question," Bill says, "and I thought even if they did, the most they would do is pull my license. I also lied to Marie about the license. I told her that since a few years had passed, I was eligible to reapply."

Bill began building an insurance business again, but less

than two years after he opened his business the California insurance board discovered the falsehood on his application and revoked his license. After that incident Bill began borrowing heavily from his friends "to keep up appearances for Marie and everyone else" until the roof finally caved in a few months later in October 1988.

Looking back on his life in Carmel, Bill can see that he continued to engage in risk-taking (or gambling) behavior even though he had quit playing poker in 1984. "I know borrowing was a gamble and applying for the license was a gamble," Bill says, "but I didn't think of it that way. To me, gambling was playing poker or betting on the horses. What I'm trying to focus on now is honesty. Mike [Brubaker] has helped me a lot with that. I've lied to people my whole life and I know I can't get things straightened out unless I quit lying. I'm lucky Marie has stuck with me through all this. I don't know where I would be today if she hadn't."

Marie Williams, a pretty woman with a beautiful, clear, olive complexion and sparkling dark eyes, has probably made much more progress in dealing with the effect of compulsive gambling on her life than her husband has. She still has a lot of anger over what's happened but she says she tries to deal with that anger constructively.

"At first, I turned that anger inward," she says, "and that was very destructive for me personally. I thought, 'How could I have been so stupid?' I never stopped to think that Bill was the one at fault, not me. I hid my anger to protect Bill because I thought he was suicidal and depressed, and I didn't want to lose him. Now, I'm supporting Bill for the right reasons—to help us build a new life together."

Marie says her daughter and some of her friends thought she should have left Bill when she found out about his gambling in Indiana. Indeed, she says, her first reaction was to flee. But upon reflection, she thought: "I believe Bill has this quirk in his nature that neither I nor anyone else understands. I love him, and I'm going to see him through this. I'm not going to leave him and throw away thirty years of marriage because he's sick." Things haven't been easy for Marie, though. She vividly remembers those dark days in Indiana when she was tired and nervous virtually all the time and found it difficult to get out of bed in the morning. The predominant feeling she had during that period was one of shame. ("I was ashamed to show my face in public," she says. "Just leaving the house was like pulling teeth for me.") All that pulled her through those days was the support of her children, her father, and counseling from a private therapist. She says Bill's spirit was so broken he was incapable of lending any support to her.

SURVIVAL FIRST, THEN PROGRESS

"All I did was survive in that first year," Marie says. "Then, I looked back on that year and said to myself, if I could make it through that, then I can make it through anything." Marie says the shock of the October 1988 debacle in Carmel passed rather quickly because she was a much stronger person than she had been eight years earlier.

"I no longer projected Bill's problems as my problems and I was able to confront Bill with my anger instead of trying to protect him," Marie says. "I know now that I have to take care of myself first before I take care of Bill or anyone else. I'm more than a mother, daughter, and wife—I'm a deserving person."

Marie says she also no longer worries about Bill as she once did. She now handles the family's finances and tries not to keep tabs on his activities. "Before, I was nervous all the time, wondering if he was going to gamble again or do something else he shouldn't be doing. I understand now that I can't possibly know what's going on in his—or anyone else's—mind. His recovery is up to him. If I don't understand something Bill is doing, I ask him about it point

blank. Bill still has difficulty answering any question directly, but he's getting better at it. We can at least talk
about things now."

Marie is still haunted by dreams of the past, but she tries
to think them through and then forget about them. She believes most of her dreams have to do with anger. "I still
carry around a lot of anger with me," she says. "I don't
think it will ever go away completely. What angers me most
is that I don't have a house I can call my own and our future
is very uncertain at a time in my life when I shouldn't have
to be worrying about the future. What I'm really doing
when I'm angry is feeling sorry for myself, and that doesn't
accomplish anything. When I find myself looking back, I
try to refocus on the present. I want to hang on to what we
have left, not mourn about the past."

Marie is very open about her and Bill's problems with
friends and acquaintances. She says she doesn't want to
waste her time building friendships with someone who may
later reject her because of Bill's history. She has discovered
that people view compulsive gamblers far differently than
they view alcoholics. "Some people will drop you like a hot
potato when they find out you're married to a compulsive
gambler," Marie says. "I've seen it happen a lot. It angers
me at first, but then I think, 'Oh, what the heck, I wouldn't
have wanted them as a friend anyway.'"

Marie reports that in general she's doing very well today.
She enjoys living in Carmel and enjoys her work as an interior decorator. "I feel better about myself today than I have
in a long time," she says. "I know I can make it and I know
Bill can, too. We are celebrating our fortieth anniversary
this year and I have a feeling it's going to be a happy one."

THE BROKEN FAMILY

U nlike Marie Williams, Jane Simms was never in the dark about her husband's gambling.

She knew almost from the beginning of their marriage that her husband, Danny, a dark, handsome, former Los Angeles police officer, was a compulsive gambler, as well as an alcoholic and drug user. Finally, four years ago, after twenty-five years of marriage, Jane divorced Danny, who reportedly is still gambling.

"I grieved tremendously for a time after our divorce," Jane Simms says, "but I didn't want him back. I knew I just couldn't take any more of his craziness."

Today, Jane attends Gam-Anon and Al-Anon (the sister organization of Alcoholics Anonymous) on a regular basis as she tries to rebuild her life after her nightmarish marriage. Outwardly, Jane appears to be doing well. She shares an expensive waterfront home in Southern California with a successful businessman she met at an Al-Anon meeting and enjoys her job as a flight attendant with a major airline.

However, she still bears the scars of the long-running ordeal with her ex-husband and frets about the damage the years of turmoil inflicted upon the couple's children,

Michelle, twenty-eight, and Mark, twenty-six. She is estranged from Mark, who blames her for the breakup with
his father, and she is concerned that Michelle is still in denial about her feelings. Jane says Michelle, a schoolteacher,
is an overachiever and a perfectionist who tries to present a
tough-minded demeanor to the outside world.

"It was hard on the kids," Jane says. "I was the only example they had, and I was always too busy trying to hold
things together to listen to them. I was not at all a creative
parent, and I know the kids missed that in their lives."

RAW EMOTIONS

Mark and Jane have had several bitter arguments since she
divorced Danny, but Mark recently began attending Adult
Children of Alcoholics meetings, leading Jane to hope that
their relationship will soon improve. "It would be so wonderful to sit down with my kids and talk this whole thing
through," Jane says. "It would be of great benefit to all of us."

Jane insists that it's therapeutic to talk about her life
with Danny, but her emotions are still raw. She is given to
displays of anger and tears as she talks about the past. As
she recalled one particularly painful attempt to reconcile
with Danny, she suddenly paused and said with a cold edge
to her voice: "Just talking about him makes me mad. I'm
tired of dealing with the assholes of the world."

In general, however, Jane seems able to cope.

"I've improved a lot in the last three years," Jane says,
"but I'm still not very trusting. I'm trying to open myself
up to intimacy and trust, but it's a slow process. When I
moved into this house with my friend, Jack, I insisted on
paying rent because I didn't want to be beholden to anyone. Jack was very understanding, but he wouldn't take
my money. He said I could set my rent money aside and
pay it to him at the end of six months if things didn't work

out. Fortunately, I didn't have to do that."

Jane still cares about what happens to her ex-husband, but more for her children's sake than her own. "My feelings for Danny died long before we were divorced," she says. "I'm terribly afraid I could see them lowering him into the ground, and I wouldn't feel anything at all."

As a step in her Gam-Anon recovery program, Jane attempted to write Danny a letter a few months ago to make amends for the things she believes she did wrong in her marriage, but reliving the past made her so angry that she tore the letter to shreds before she had finished. "I was writing the letter for myself," she says, "but I simply couldn't bring myself to ask him for forgiveness for anything. Maybe someday I will be able to, but not now. At least I can laugh and cry about these things with my friends in Gam-Anon and Al-Anon, and that makes me feel much, much better."

Jane is only now beginning to feel like a full woman again. "For years," she says, "I was just a functional woman running on automatic pilot. I had no feelings at all. I had lost my sexuality, my femininity, and my ability to be a loving mother to my children. During the height of his craziness, Danny became impotent, and we didn't have sex for a period of six years. In the meantime, he was out chasing prostitutes and young girls. I don't know if he was able to have sex with them, but it certainly didn't make me feel very attractive or desirable."

Jane, a small, attractive forty-nine-year-old woman with short brown hair, has a much stronger image of herself today. "Looking back I can see Danny was probably addicted to sex, just like he was everything else, and his impotence was probably caused by guilt. I never should have permitted things he did to color how I felt about myself, but I did."

Jane and Danny began dating in high school and got married after Jane discovered she was pregnant. "Danny was an outgoing person who liked to play the field, and I doubt he would have married me if I hadn't gotten pregnant. For years, I felt guilty about that, and I think Danny took advantage of my guilt," Jane says.

Things never went smoothly for the couple. Danny worked for a short time for Jane's father, who was a building contractor, but he soon tired of that and joined the Los Angeles Police Department. Being a police officer suited Danny's life-style. He worked odd hours and drank and gambled in his off-hours with friends from the force. His principal after-hours hangouts were the card clubs of Gardena, where he liked to play lowball.

N U M B E R - O N E   P R I O R I T Y

Jane recalls Danny coming home late one night and telling her that he had lost his paycheck gambling. She asked him what they were going to do for money. He nonchalantly told her not to worry about it; he would roll a drunk or something to get some money.

Jane knew Danny was always in trouble with his superiors for tardiness and attitude problems, but she was surprised when he came home early one day and announced he had quit the force.

"I think he quit before they fired him," Jane says. "I believe they knew he was always late for duty because of gambling and that he was working some type of scam with prostitutes. Danny must have quit at least twenty jobs while we were married. The only time I remember him being fired from a job was when he was caught stealing at this place where he worked as a security manager. He went berserk when they fired him and he claimed it was a frame-up."

After leaving the police force, Danny held a variety of outside sales jobs, even though some of them didn't last more than a few weeks. "Danny was a great con artist," Jane says. "He was very good-looking when he was younger and very charming. I think he could talk anyone into hiring him. He never wanted a regular nine-to-five job. That wouldn't give him enough freedom to come and go as he pleased. He needed freedom to gamble. Gambling was always his number-one priority."

Jane was always available to bail out the family when Danny was out of work or when he had written bad checks to cover gambling losses. She worked throughout their marriage, sometimes holding down two jobs to make ends meet. She also took in ironing and hid the money she made so Danny couldn't find it.

"I know I enabled Danny, but I didn't know what else to do," Jane says. "We had two children who needed love and support, and I felt I needed to be the Rock of Gibraltar for the family. I also loved Danny. He could con me, too. He could be very sweet and considerate. When he did something wrong, he would always be very apologetic and promise to do better in the future. I really thought that he needed me and that eventually he would change."

Throughout the first half of their marriage, Jane regarded Danny as a loveable screw-up who gambled and drank too much. She says that she was caught up in a fantasy world of youth and happiness in which everything would work out all right in the end. Then, suddenly, after about fifteen years of marriage, Danny's personality changed. He became violent and paranoid and began bullying her and the children, who were then in their early teens.

"Everything was a nightmare from that point on," Jane says. "He was using speed, drinking heavily, and leaving home for days at a time. When he was home, we were always arguing, and I never knew what he was going to do next. Once, when we were arguing in our bedroom, he began beating and kicking me, and Michelle ran in the room to try to stop him. Danny called her 'a little cunt' and chased her down the hallway and dragged her back in our room. Then he looked at me and said, 'See, Jane, look what you made me do.'"

Danny hit the children on at least two other occasions, and once when Jane locked him out of the house, he broke the windows and drove off in her car. Jane was frightened. "I knew Danny always had firearms, and I was afraid he was going to kill us or himself."

The madness began to take a toll on Jane both mentally and physically. She developed a painful foot condition, which her doctor said could have been caused by stress, and she began to think she was losing her mind. "I visualized my sanity as a rope which was being pulled tighter and tighter," she says. "It was a scary feeling. I thought about suicide, but I don't think I could have ever killed myself because of the children. I decided to shut off my feelings completely as a matter of survival."

Mark and Michelle were also experiencing difficulties. Mark's schoolwork suffered, and Michelle cut down on her outside activities and stayed around home more. Jane tearfully recalls one especially poignant scene, in which Mark, in an attempt to catch up with his schoolwork, studied by the light of a kerosene lamp after their electricity had been cut off for nonpayment of a bill.

U N F U L F I L L E D   H O P E

In 1980, Jane decided that the only possible solution to their mutual problem was for Danny to stop drinking. She called a San Pedro, California, alcoholism treatment center near their home and arranged for a conference with an alcoholism counselor. The counselor was Mike Brubaker.

With Jane's help, Mike set up an intervention in which he and Jane confronted Danny about his drinking and drug use, and much to Jane's surprise, Danny agreed to enter treatment. Mike also suggested to Danny that he look into his gambling habits while he was in treatment.

Jane participated in the family component of the treatment program and began attending Al-Anon meetings. She thought her troubles were over. She found that Al-Anon provided answers to her problems and began attending several meetings a week at the hospital and elsewhere. She also believed the treatment program would turn Danny around.

She was wrong on the second score. "I think Danny just went through the motions," Jane says. "He was always criticizing something about the treatment program, and he looked down his nose at Mike. He said, 'He's nothing but a horse player. What does he know?' "

Danny seemed improved, however, and after he completed treatment, he attended four Gamblers Anonymous and Gam-Anon meetings with Jane. "I don't think Danny wanted to go to the meetings, but I was encouraged that he was at least willing to try," Jane recalls. "But after the fourth meeting, he said he didn't belong there and never went back."

Jane continues to be close to Mike Brubaker, who, she says, has been a great source of support in her recovery. "Mike would have helped Danny, too," Jane says, "but Danny rejected his help."

Mike remembers Danny angrily denied he had a problem with gambling. "Danny wouldn't listen to me or to anyone else," Mike says. "I finally gave up on him. I told him he knew how to get hold of me or someone else in GA if he ever decided he needed help."

Several months after Danny completed alcohol and drug treatment, the craziness returned. On one occasion, Danny went to Las Vegas for a couple of days and returned home with two underage girls whom he said he was taking to the Long Beach Grand Prix auto race, and later, he took a girlfriend to the bank with him to pose as his wife and forge Jane's signature on a loan.

Jane finally threw in the towel. She told Danny he had to move out. She took the added step of declaring personal bankruptcy so she could disassociate herself from Danny's debts and protect their house from foreclosure.

Danny went quietly at first, but soon began begging Jane for another chance. She finally agreed to let him come back home, but she warned him that this was absolutely his last chance. The day after she reconciled with Danny, Jane spent the day alone in her bedroom. She says she cried for hours and hours.

HOLDING FIRM

The reconciliation was short-lived. Within a month, Danny went to Gardena to play poker and didn't return for a few days. He was driving a cab at the time, and the cab company had to retrieve the cab from the taxi zone in front of a card club. Jane put Danny's belongings in the garage, and when he returned home, she told him to get his things out of the garage and leave. Jane recalls that she and Danny had a "bit of a tussle," but that he left without too much argument. After a couple of days, Danny began begging Jane to take him back again, but she held firm. Then the harassment began. One particularly chilling episode occurred when Danny cut in front of Jane's car as she and Michelle were leaving a parking lot near their home and attempted to run Michelle down when she got out of the car. After that scare, Jane obtained a restraining order and had Danny arrested when he showed up at the house the next day.

"He kept harassing me for a while," Jane says, "but every time he turned up, I had him thrown in jail. I knew I couldn't let him off the hook again because every time I did, I wound up paying the price for it."

Danny finally gave up pursuit, and when Jane filed for divorce, he didn't contest it. He didn't even show up in court on the day the divorce was granted. "I cried when it was finally over," Jane says, "but I knew I couldn't go on. I had a life to live, and I couldn't live it with Danny. He was draining the life out of me."

Shortly after her divorce, Jane Simms took a job as a flight attendant for the airline where she had worked in the reservations department for a number of years. She enjoys flying and attends Al-Anon and Gam-Anon meetings both at home and on her travels. Jane and Danny had very few friends when they were married, but now she has a wide circle of friends, both inside and outside of self-help groups. "I never knew how important friends were," she says.

She says many people don't understand how she stayed in a bad marriage for so long, and at times, she doesn't either. "Danny wasn't the only one at fault," she says. "I was at fault, too, for enabling him to remain the way he was. His parents were both compulsive gamblers, so he had two strikes against him when he started. My great mistake was making things easy for him and hurting the children in the process. I thought I was being a good wife and mother by staying in the marriage, but I wasn't. I should have removed the children from that situation."

Jane saw Danny in the summer of 1989 when he dropped by to inform her that he was getting married. He told her things were going well for him and that he was no longer drinking. Jane said for the first time since their divorce she felt sorry for Danny. "He looked really bad," she says. "His face was puffy, he needed dental work and he was losing his hair. I doubt seriously that he's quit drinking, and I know from friends that he's still gambling."

If Jane felt any sympathy for Danny, it was short-lived, because as he was leaving, Danny made a remark with which Jane took offense. She shouted after him: "Just remember, Danny, when you die, I'm the one who's going to get your Social Security—not your new wife. I've earned it."

Jane laughs when she tells that story. "I guess you might say that I've still got a little anger in me."

16

LIFE WITH A COMPULSIVE GAMBLER

At least three people were struggling at the Thursday-night meeting of compulsive gamblers in Monterey in March 1990. A pleasant young man in his thirties admitted point blank that he didn't know what choice he would make the following morning when he was faced with the decision of going to work or hitting a satellite gambling establishment for a racetrack in the area. Another man at the meeting had gambled on Monday and another was fighting a burning compulsion to gamble after an on-again, off-again battle of several years.

According to treatment experts, all three men could be candidates for formal treatment for compulsive gambling because of their continued inability to stop gambling even after they have acknowledged their problem.

Following the Thursday night Monterey meeting, one of the men who had been struggling acknowledged that he would like to seek professional help, but said he couldn't afford it. Interestingly, the $7,000 he had lost in his last big gambling binge would have covered much of the cost for a full course of treatment in one twenty-eight-day hospital program. The man had always been resourceful in obtaining money to gamble, but he said: "I'm tapped out now. I wouldn't know where to lay my hands on money for treatment."

Mike Brubaker estimates that half of the people at the Thursday night compulsive gamblers meeting would benefit enormously from formalized treatment. Although he has relied solely on the power of a self-help program in his eleven years of recovery from compulsive gambling, Mike doesn't believe self-help programs are substitutes for treatment. He believes that treatment is frequently a prerequisite for many people seeking to abstain from gambling through Gamblers Anonymous and the Twelve Step process.

"I think of self-help as a complement to treatment," Mike says. "I don't think the retention rate in Gamblers Anonymous is ever going to improve dramatically unless we have a better treatment system."

THE NEED FOR FORMAL TREATMENT

Mike bases his views on what has transpired in the alcoholism treatment field in the last ten or fifteen years. He attributes the rapid growth of Alcoholics Anonymous in the last few years to the fact that large numbers of people are entering AA as a result of treatment and early intervention into their drinking problems.

"Most people usually have to hit bottom before they are ready for Alcoholics Anonymous or Gamblers Anonymous. Even the founders of AA didn't think anyone was ready for recovery until they hit bottom," Mike says. "Unfortunately, a lot of people die on their way to the bottom, and others can't get off the bottom once they reach it because all of their support systems are gone. They have nothing left—no family, no friends, no job, no one who cares about them. That's why treatment and intervention are necessary."

Fifteen years into his recovery from alcoholism, Mike doesn't know to this day whether he would have been able to turn his life around without formal intervention into his alcohol problem by the U.S. Navy. "I frankly don't know if I would be alive today without the help of the Navy treatment program. And I don't know whether some of our former patients, like Mrs. Ford, Senator Talmadge, Billy Carter, or Buzz Aldrin, would have gotten sober without intervention and treatment. I don't think GA alone would have been enough for Alex Petros or Barbara Cummings. Without treatment, I think both of them would still be out there gambling today.

"We need more treatment resources in this country if we are ever going to make a dent in the compulsive gambling problem."

Mike points out that even with treatment and a large AA and self-help network, only fifteen to twenty percent of all alcoholics ever receive help. And the percentage is obviously much lower for compulsive gamblers. "It's more like one percent—if that," Mike estimates.

Mike Brubaker's comparison of the current state of treatment for alcoholism and compulsive gambling is an apt one, according to California psychologist Dr. Dewey Jacobs.

Jacobs says compulsive gambling is "the last of the major addictions remaining to be addressed in this country." He says that the public is keenly aware of the harmful effects of alcohol, drugs, smoking, and overeating and that treatment or some type of professional assistance is readily available for all of these addictions. That's not the case with compulsive gambling, Jacobs says.

"We have a tremendous shortage of treatment resources for compulsive gambling," he says, "but hopefully, we are at the threshold of a new frontier in education, prevention, and treatment."

Jacobs says the shortage of treatment resources for compulsive gambling roughly parallels the state of the alcoholism treatment field twenty or thirty years ago. At that time, alcoholism treatment for the most part was excluded from the mainstream of the U.S. health care delivery system. Few physicians or psychologists had the expertise—or even the desire—to treat alcoholism, and very few private hospitals admitted alcoholic patients, much less provided specialized treatment.

One of the pioneers of alcoholism treatment, sixty-seven-year-old Dr. Max A. Schneider of Laguna Beach, California, recalls that in the 1960s he once had to offer a small bribe to a nurse to get an alcoholic patient admitted to a general hospital in California. "I told her if she would agree to admit him, I would buy her dinner at the most expensive restaurant in town if my patient caused any more trouble than any other patient on her unit."

Today, hospitals compete for alcoholic patients. There are presently more than 7,700 public and private alcohol and chemical dependency treatment programs in the United States, and because of the efforts of Schneider and others in the American Society of Addiction Medicine, more than 3,600 physicians and psychiatrists are now certified as specialists in the treatment of alcoholism and drug dependency.

TRIAL AND ERROR

For the same expansion to occur in the treatment of compulsive gambling, Jacobs believes four things have to happen: increased public awareness of the problem; public acceptance of compulsive gambling as a treatable illness; extensive development of treatment resources by public agencies; and increased pressure on insurance companies and other third-party payors to include coverage for compulsive gambling treatment in their health care policies. The last step, according to Jacobs, is essential for the development of crucial private-sector treatment resources, which presently account for the majority of all alcoholism treatment programs in the United States.

The few compulsive gambling programs that exist today usually provide treatment under a different diagnosis, such as depression or substance abuse, to qualify for reimbursement under the patient's insurance policy. Jacobs says it is very rare for pathological gambling to be covered as a primary diagnosis, even though it has been included in the American Psychiatric Association's *Diagnostic and Statistical Manual of Mental Disorders* since 1980.

Jacobs says that hospitals that have opened programs exclusively for compulsive gambling have fared poorly because of reimbursement problems. The current trend is for hospitals providing treatment to assign gambling patients to drug and alcohol or psychiatric treatment units within the hospital. It's less than a perfect system, but at present, Jacobs and his colleagues welcome any system that adds to the nation's treatment resources.

Compounding the present problem, Jacobs says, is the fact that only a handful of clinicians are skilled in the diagnosis and treatment of compulsive gambling. He adds, "To my knowledge, no physician, no psychiatrist, no psychologist, no social worker, no marriage and family counselor has ever received formal graduate training on compulsive gambling treatment. Everything we've learned thus far has been by trial and error."

Jacobs believes, however, that the tide is already beginning to turn and that within the next five or ten years, there will be a solid base of treatment resources in the United States. "There is a much wider acceptance of the problem of compulsive gambling today than there was only a couple of years ago," Jacobs says, "and I believe better insurance coverage for treatment may be just around the corner. Historically, the pressure for adequate insurance coverage for a particular condition begins to build when the public accepts that there indeed is a problem and that adequate treatment can help correct it."

He also notes that at least a half dozen states are now offering training for treatment professionals, including New Jersey, which has begun a certification program for counselors. "I believe we will be all right within the next few years," Jacobs says, "but it hasn't been an easy struggle, particularly in my home state of California. We should be leading the way in California since our citizens spend more on gambling than any other state. Instead we're bringing up the rear. That's been very disappointing and frustrating to me personally."

California, with 26 million people, currently has few treatment resources for compulsive gambling. In fact, until 1990, when CPC Westwood Hospital in Los Angeles opened an inpatient program under the direction of Dr. Richard Rosenthal, the nearest private hospital-based compulsive gambling program had been Charter Hospital of Las Vegas. Prior to 1990, the only other treatment programs in the state were the federally funded Naval Hospitals in Long Beach and Oakland, and the Veterans Administration Hospital at Loma Linda, which had been treating a limited number of patients.

With the exception of the Rimrock Foundation program in Billings, Montana, Charter Hospital of Las Vegas, CPC Westwood Hospital, and perhaps one or two other programs, most hospital programs for compulsive gambling are located east of the Mississippi. These programs include the venerable Brecksville, Ohio, Veterans Administration program which was founded in 1972; Taylor Manor in Ellicott City, Maryland, where Barbara Cummings underwent treatment in 1986; the National Center for Pathological Gambling in Baltimore; Valley Forge Hospital in Pennsylvania; and South Oaks Hospital in Amityville, New York, which developed the South Oaks Gambling Screen for the assessment of patients. There are other Veterans Administration programs in Miami, Florida; Bay Pines, Florida; Lyons, New

Jersey; Brooklyn, New York; the New Hope Foundation in Marlboro, New Jersey; and the Philadelphia Psychiatric Institute. Other programs are scattered throughout New York, New England, and the Mid-Atlantic states.

The great majority of the hospital programs are in psychiatric hospitals that are equipped to deal with the major depression and suicidal tendencies that so often accompany compulsive gambling disorders. One of the few gambling programs in a nonpsychiatric hospital setting is the Rimrock Foundation in Billings, Montana.

Building a Successful Program

The nonprofit Rimrock Foundation program, which was launched four years ago in consultation with Dr. Robert Custer, the founder of the Brecksville, Ohio, VA program, attracts patients from Montana, the Northwest, and Canada for a twenty-eight-day residential program in which compulsive gamblers are treated along with patients suffering from other addictive disorders. The forty-one-bed Rimrock center also provides treatment for alcoholism, drug dependency, eating disorders (bulimia and anorexia nervosa), and sexual addiction.

One of the hallmarks of the Rimrock program is its relatively low cost—$6,900 for a twenty-eight-day stay, plus an additional $250 in psychiatric fees, if needed. The cost in most cases is less than half that for comparable lengths of stay in psychiatric hospitals.

Associate Director Mona L. Sumner, the charter board president of the twenty-two-year-old Rimrock Foundation, said Rimrock decided to institute a compulsive gambling program following the legalization of gambling in the state of Montana. She says the Rimrock staff correctly predicted that there would be an upshot of compulsive gambling in the state and believed that the foundation should assume a leadership role in dealing with the anticipated increase in gambling.

At first, only a trickle of patients in the Rimrock program had a primary diagnosis of compulsive gambling, but last year almost 6 percent of the patients had a primary gambling diagnosis, including a substantial number of women. Many other Rimrock patients with multiple addictions are also compulsive gamblers, Sumner says.

Rimrock's program, like most of the other compulsive gambling programs in the United States, is based upon the Twelve Step principles of GA, which emphasize total abstinence from gambling and stress that recovery is a life-long process. The Rimrock staff includes two recovering compulsive gamblers.

The Rimrock program consists of intensive education and therapy for what Sumner describes as the "common core psychology of addiction"—psychological dependency, mental obsession, emotional compulsion, and "the complex pattern of safeguarding behaviors that hide the reality of the illness from both the patient and family." Families of patients also participate in the program, and patients are required to attend a three-month aftercare program upon completion of inpatient treatment.

The Rimrock Foundation also provides treatment on an outpatient basis for patients not requiring hospitalization and plays host to a number of GA and Gam-Anon meetings.

Sumner says that Rimrock hasn't experienced the full brunt of reimbursement constraints felt by some of its sister programs in the United States because of its relatively low cost, but she and the foundation are lobbying the Montana State Gambling Commission for set-asides from gambling revenues to finance treatment for patients who can't afford it and for education and prevention efforts in the state.

Sumner believes that since the state licenses gambling and receives revenues from it, the state has the responsibility to fund education, prevention and treatment activities. "Since we've legalized gambling in Montana, the compulsive gambling problem has gotten much worse," she says. "There are a lot of heavy gamblers in Billings and throughout the state. What really concerns us is that we are seeing a very high percentage of women gamblers from Montana. I think the escape provided by gambling is very appealing to some women."

On a per capita basis, despite the increase in gambling, Montana is served very well. Billings, the picturesque city where the Rimrock Foundation is located, has a population of only 70,000, and Montana itself is the seventh least populous state in the nation with less than 800,000 inhabitants.

Not all compulsive gamblers, of course, require hospitalization. In fact, Dr. Richard Rosenthal believes most compulsive gamblers can be treated as outpatients. He'll consider an inpatient hospital program for the gambler who is significantly depressed or suicidal, or whose recovery is complicated by other serious addictions or psychopathology. He will also consider hospitalization when there is a lack of external support, if the gambler is physically and/or mentally exhausted, if the gambler is contemplating a crime or some other potentially disastrous alternative, or if repeated attempts to stop gambling have been unsuccessful. He notes, however, that most compulsive gamblers are able to stop when actively involved in GA, or when their omnipotence and denial are aggressively confronted in the first few outpatient therapy sessions.

Rosenthal's sessions take place in a subdued lamplit office on Roxbury Drive in Beverly Hills, a couple of blocks west of the glitzy boutiques of Rodeo Drive. Despite the upscale address, Rosenthal's patients come from all walks of life. Rosenthal himself hardly fits the Beverly Hills stereotype. He is a serious, professorial man who prefers tweed jackets and conservative suits to designer clothes. He usually catches lunch on the run at the small coffee shop on the first floor of his building.

• • •

PATIENT PROFILE

His patients generally fit into three loosely defined groups. The first group consists of those who are new to therapy. They may have been referred by an Employee Assistance professional at their place of employment, a lawyer or the courts, or brought in by a family member.

Rosenthal says these patients are sometimes naive with regard to gambling problems. They may be unaware of the nature of their problem and may think of their problem as unique. He says many of them had no idea where to turn for help, and if they had heard of GA—and a surprising number had not—it was only just recently, and some had ruled it out for one reason or another. Some of those who are new to therapy are coerced into treatment against their will, Rosenthal says, usually by their family or the courts. However, despite their initial opposition, many do well, he says. Rosenthal doesn't believe it is necessary for a gambler to bottom out, or seek help on his own to respond to treatment. He says there are ways to engage reluctant patients in therapy. However, if he finds that he is not getting anywhere with a patient, he'll discuss it with the patient and either recommend some changes or discontinue treatment. He says that he doesn't believe "it is in anyone's interest to continue a treatment that isn't going anywhere."

He categorizes a second group of patients as treatment veterans. Some are referred by other therapists for consultation or have gone through inpatient programs in other parts of the country. Some of these patients have been in therapy for years but have never mentioned their gambling to their therapist, or perhaps their therapist was inexperienced in dealing with the compulsive gambler. He says more than a few of these patients had been chronically lying to their therapist.

The third and perhaps largest group consists of those who have been attending GA, in some cases for many years, but have been unable to put together any significant period of abstinence. Those in this group may have succeeded in stopping gambling, only to recognize they had other problems, such as depression or problems with relationships. They may have become aware of other self-destructive patterns.

Rosenthal always initiates the treatment process with a thorough evaluation, which enables him to determine the nature and severity of the gambling problem, other areas of impaired functioning, methods of coping and general personality. Diagnosing the gambling problem is the easy part, Rosenthal says. "What requires skill and experience on the part of the therapist is deciding what the optimal conditions for therapy are: how much structure does the patient need to be able to stay in treatment and benefit? This structure and the treatment setting is different for each patient. For example, how often does the patient need to be seen? Should he be seen as an outpatient, or go into the hospital, or perhaps a halfway house? Should he be treated in his community or out of state? Should the family be involved in the therapy and in what way? Should the spouse be seen separately, perhaps even by another counselor or therapist, or should the patient and spouse be seen together? Is medication called for? If the right setting and structure can be provided so that there is a good fit, practically every compulsive gambler should be able to be treated successfully."

IMPORTANCE OF GA

Regardless of which treatment regimen Rosenthal recommends, he urges his patients to participate in GA. "If they're not going to GA, I ask them why, and I analyze it. And I may keep bringing the subject up during the course of treatment. It's frequently the only clue to their denial of their problem, or their belief that they are better than other compulsive gamblers, for example, or different. I've seen only a few gamblers who just couldn't bring themselves to go to GA, and an important part of their therapy was helping them to get there. One young man, for example, had a serious social phobia, and he had to get healthier before he could go to a meeting."

Involvement in GA is more than simply meetings. Rosenthal stresses that recovering gamblers need to participate actively in the GA program: "It's not enough to sit in the back of the room and say nothing. Speaking at meetings, getting a sponsor, working the [Twelve] Steps—being involved is what's important. GA is a wonderful program that's completely consistent and complementary with what takes place in psychotherapy. Gamblers learn to accept their limitations, to be honest with themselves—not just about their gambling, but in their relationships and especially with regard to their feelings—and to practice responsibility." There is only one area in which Rosenthal's treatment philosophy differs from the GA program. "GA teaches that it's not important to understand why one gambles. I understand why they stress that, and for the majority of gamblers it may be true. However, there are those who need to know why they gamble in order to achieve abstinence. For many, gambling-free periods only lead to a sense of futility. Nothing has changed in their lives, they don't feel any better—if anything, they feel worse. They inevitably return to gambling."

Central to Rosenthal's understanding of compulsive gambling is the concept of omnipotence, which he defines as "an illusion of power and control which defends against intolerable feelings, most particularly helplessness, depression, guilt, or shame." He cites as an example the case of a man who had grown up being constantly compared to an older brother who had died tragically in childhood. When he received good grades in school, for example, his mother would become nostalgic about how smart his brother had been and what he could have achieved if only he had lived.

He felt he was fighting a ghost, and that nothing he did was ever good enough to please his parents. In later life, the man would start to achieve some success, but would then sink into depression. Gambling offered a threefold solution for him: It allowed him an escape, a way of not having to think about such problems; it offered an opportunity to win big—just the kind of spectacular success which would finally impress his parents; and it was a way of acting out his anger at his parents for not ever really loving him.

These underlying problems had to be addressed before the man could achieve recovery, Rosenthal says. Once the gambler has stopped gambling, and only then, can he begin working on self-esteem issues. Rosenthal is convinced that all compulsive gamblers have low self-esteem, and that it precedes the gambling problem. Therapy, as he describes it, focuses on learning to tolerate and accept feelings, unravel various patterns of self-deception, sort out confused boundaries, and develop a capacity for realistic and obtainable goals.

Education in relapse prevention is also an important part of therapy, Rosenthal says. "The patient must learn that slips [or relapses] don't just happen, but that there is a whole series of events, or bad choices, leading up to them. It's difficult for people to accept that there are always consequences to their actions—not just sometimes, and not just because I or someone else says so." He views the role of the therapist as removing blocks to the natural growth of the individual, and, he says, "once back on track, it's largely a matter for most people of practice and developing good habits. Recovery is a twenty-four-hour-a-day proposition. Everyone has choices all day, and if you do the right thing you feel better about yourself and if you do something hurtful, you're going to feel worse. It gets very simple." Reaching that point and believing it, however, is the difficult part for compulsive gamblers, and frequently requires the help of a therapist, as well as active, ongoing participation in GA.

RECOVERING
IN LAS VEGAS

It may seem ironic to some people that the first hospital treatment program for compulsive gamblers in the western United States is located within eyesight of the great hotels and casinos lining the famous Las Vegas Strip.

But one native resident doesn't think it's strange at all.

"We need a program here because the compulsive gambling problem appears to be worse here than elsewhere," says Dr. Robert Hunter, clinical director of the Charter Hospital of Las Vegas compulsive gambling unit. The problem is worse, he says, because of the availability of gambling in Las Vegas and the lure of the city to gamblers from all over the country.

"My belief is that we tend to attract gamblers rather than create them," Hunter says. "Las Vegas is a very transient community. It's easy to find work here, the climate is good, and gambling is available twenty-four hours a day. Most of our patients are gamblers who have relocated to Las Vegas from somewhere else. We've had only two Las Vegas natives in treatment in the three years we have been in operation."

Hunter calls his hometown a living research lab for compulsive gambling and believes it is the ideal proving ground for clinicians and researchers with an interest in compulsive gambling. The thirty-four-year-old psychologist says he loves working with compulsive gamblers. "I've seen some dramatic turnarounds by people who were in a total state of collapse when I first saw them," Hunter says. "There's a ton of work that needs to be done in this field, but I believe people in this community and others are beginning to recognize that compulsive gambling is a disease that can be diagnosed and treated successfully. There is a groundswell of recovery developing in Las Vegas both through Gamblers Anonymous, which is very strong here, and through our program. As a matter of fact, I believe Las Vegas is the best place in the world to get well."

MODEST SUCCESS

Charter Hospital of Las Vegas, part of the nationwide Charter Medical Corporation hospital chain headquartered in Macon, Georgia, opened its compulsive gambling unit three years ago, and the flow of patients into the unit has been modest but fairly steady. The average number of compulsive gamblers in treatment at any given time is seven or eight patients who stay for periods ranging from three to seven weeks, depending upon the severity of other problems associated with their gambling disorder. Issues concurrent with compulsive gambling range from bipolar (or manic-depressive) disorders and severe depression to chronic alcohol- and drug-abuse conditions. All patients in the gambling program are dual-diagnosis patients, which means they have at least one other psychiatric diagnosis in addition to compulsive (or pathological) gambling.

As Hunter noted, the majority of the patients in the unit are people who are drawn to Las Vegas by the allure of gambling. About a third of the patients are from out of state, some from as far away as the East Coast or Midwest. Some of the out-of-state patients are referred by other Charter hospitals throughout the nation, and others are attracted to the program because of its national reputation, which in large measure is due to the late Dr. Robert Custer's association with the unit as a consultant.

One of the out-of-state patients recently treated at Charter was a professional football player whose promising career had been short-circuited by compulsive gambling in the early 1980s. He had undergone treatment previously, but had resumed gambling. He was treated in Las Vegas and took up temporary residence in the city so he could benefit from the city's strong GA support system.

"He doesn't have a GA support system near his home in the South," Hunter says, "and I believe it's very difficult for someone to recover without that support—particularly in the early stages of recovery."

Hunter, who has treated a couple of professional baseball players in addition to the football player, says that because of their great competitive drive, athletes are a high-risk group. Both he and Dr. Richard Rosenthal note, however, that it is rare for an athlete with a compulsive gambling problem to achieve the status of a Pete Rose since the gambling usually interferes with their performance. Even Rose acknowledged in a statement given in connection with his income tax case in Ohio that he had not begun gambling excessively until his active career as a player had ended.

INDUSTRY SUPPORT

In addition to out-of-state patients and athletes, a significant group of patients undergoing treatment in Las Vegas is gaming industry employees. Compulsive gambling, as well as other addictive behavior, is a significant problem in the casino industry, according to Hunter. Gaming industry employees with compulsive gambling problems move to Las Vegas to get jobs in the casinos so they can be close to the action, Hunter says.

A young craps dealer at a casino in Lake Tahoe, Nevada, observes: "Every night, workers from other casinos come to our casino to play when they get off work. You can set your clock by them. They are not there to have fun. They'll come on a regular basis for a while and then disappear. Some of them move on to other casinos, and others leave town, maybe for Las Vegas or somewhere else."

The dealer says workers at casinos usually know who the compulsive gamblers are in their ranks and tend to shy away from them. "They are nothing but trouble," he says. "We refer to them as 'sickos.' When a gambler comes in from another casino, we'll pass the word along that the 'sicko' is here again."

Hunter says the casinos in Las Vegas are very supportive of the Charter treatment program. He cites Stephen Wynn, the flamboyant owner of the Golden Nugget and the Mirage, as being especially supportive. Wynn has an employee assistance program for employees who need help for gambling or drug/alcohol problems and "sets a real clear direction for his employees," Hunter says. "He educates them about compulsive gambling and makes every attempt to see that his employees get help if they need it. The Nugget and Mirage both list Gamblers Anonymous meetings in their hotel directories, which I'm not sure anyone else does."

Hunter says most patients have suffered a total emotional collapse prior to admission. They may be suicidal, or may have attempted suicide, or be so acutely depressed that they've lost their ability to function. As a result, most of the patients are admitted to the hospital's psychiatric unit and are not transferred to the compulsive gambling program until their condition has stabilized. Many of the patients with acute psychiatric problems are in treatment six to seven weeks.

Once the patients are admitted to the compulsive gambling unit, they participate in an intensive rehabilitation program consisting of individual and group therapy, educational lectures, recreational therapy, family therapy, and GA meetings. The hospital portion of treatment is followed by twelve months of aftercare, in which the patient returns to the hospital on an outpatient basis once a week for group therapy.

"Our patients follow a grueling schedule," Hunter says. "We keep them busy from eight in the morning until nine at night while they are here." Treatment is individually tailored. "We assemble whatever therapies are needed for an individual patient. We may use Gestalt therapy, or include someone in a special group for men or women. We draw from a full range of therapies in our adult psychiatric program, as well as our addictions program."

Intensive one-on-one therapy usually takes place in the early stages of treatment, Hunter says, as he and the other counselors attempt to impress upon patients the need for them to confront the reality of their disease and come clean about the extent of their gambling. This stage of treatment usually is a drawing-out process that may last up to several days.

"Compulsive gamblers tend to put on a good show," Hunter says. "They are masters of con, and with time they start to buy the bullshit they're spewing. All the time, of course, they are feeling rejected or slighted by others, and are killing themselves because they are totally out of touch with their feelings and what's going on with them. One of my primary goals in treatment is to get the patient to recognize there's a good person inside them that the gambling is hiding and destroying."

• • •

D I F F E R E N T   T R E A T M E N T — S A M E   G O A L

Hunter, who received his undergraduate degree in psychology at the University of Nevada–Las Vegas and his doctorate in psychology from the University of Nevada–Reno, began working in the alcohol and drug addiction field as a private practitioner following graduation but soon found himself being drawn to treating compulsive gamblers, many of whom were dually addicted to alcohol or drugs. "These gamblers kept showing up in my practice," he says, "and I became totally fascinated with the dynamics of compulsive gambling." He believes the treatment of compulsive gambling is "completely dissimilar" from that for alcoholism or drug dependency. In treating gamblers, he says it is "necessary to figure out what feelings they are blocking with the gambling." He says that's generally not true with alcohol or drug patients, most of whom don't need to know why they drink or use in order to recover. The goal of both alcohol/drug and compulsive gambling treatment is the same, however—total abstinence.

Hunter continues to maintain a private practice not far from the hospital where he counsels compulsive gamblers on a one-on-one basis. He describes the private therapy process as "very feeling-related." As a rule, the patients he counsels in his private practice are not in crisis and don't suffer from a severe coexisting psychiatric condition. Like Dr. Richard Rosenthal, Hunter believes the preferred method of treatment for the majority of compulsive gamblers is outpatient therapy, supplemented by heavy involvement in GA.

Howie Cornbleth, a recovering compulsive gambler with eighteen years abstinence, manages the compulsive gambling unit at the hospital on a day to day basis, but Hunter is usually on the unit for several hours each day including most weekends. Hunter is a friendly, energetic redhead who dresses casually in sneakers, sport shirts, and cotton pants. At 6 feet, 5 inches, he towers over his patients, but he is an informal individual and hardly an intimidating figure. Hunter says he remembers the story of each gambler who has gone through the Charter program and points with pride to a number of patients who have totally turned their lives around following treatment. "I've seen some real miraculous recoveries in the last three years," he says. "The patients we see in the program are really hurting by the time they get here and recovery for them is usually a very difficult process. Our success rate is about 50 percent, which is very good considering the condition most of our patients are in."

He says about one-quarter of the patients who check into the Charter program are suicidal and that a number of them have attempted suicide. Hunter says some of the crisis calls he receives "would break your heart."

He cites the case of an oil field worker on the Gulf Coast who called him late one night after watching a sports program on ESPN in which Roy Firestone interviewed Hunter about compulsive gambling.

"The Firestone interview probably saved that man's life," Rob Hunter says. "He had tuned in to ESPN to check the scores of games he had bet on and just caught the end of Roy Firestone's interview with me. He had a shotgun and intended to kill himself if he lost again. He called me instead, and I talked him through the crisis and convinced him to come into treatment. It's a good thing he called me because he lost heavily that night."

He also has received calls from people in jail and from people in other parts of the country who at first refuse to identify themselves. "These are real human dramas," he says.

COMING OUT OF THE CLOSET

Many of the Charter patients have been in therapy of one type or another prior to entering treatment but very few of them have been diagnosed as compulsive gamblers. "There is a lot of naivete about compulsive gambling—even in Las Vegas. It's a disease that is still in the closet. Many therapists overlook compulsive gambling in the evaluation process," Hunter says. He adds that the patients, too, are usually unaware of the true nature of their problems. Less than half of them have ever been to a GA meeting, and most of them did not know compulsive gambling was a specific psychiatric disorder.

While many Charter patients engage in casino gambling or sports betting and are frequently addicted to either drugs or alcohol, a surprising number of patients are big-time speculators in the commodities markets, Hunter says. Furthermore, about half the patients from Las Vegas are females.

Whatever the game, gambling is not a disease of money, Hunter says. "We had one man in here who had lost $10 million in two years, and a young woman who had lost only $800 in six months. The woman was just as devastated as the man who had lost the $10 million."

Most of the patients Hunter treats at Charter "leave here in a pretty good spot," he says. "After they leave here, though, their health belongs to them. They own what's inside them and if they continue to be honest with themselves and work a good GA program, then they are going to be all right."

One of the central components of the Charter compulsive gambling program is Dr. Rob Hunter's Friday afternoon group therapy session for current and former patients.

It's a lively, freewheeling, ninety-minute session, full of laughter and tears, which Hunter obviously relishes and looks forward to each week as a means of assessing the progress of his patients, old and new.

• • •

HAVE, DO, ARE

On a warm November day in 1989, a dozen people, including seven current patients, four of whom were from out of state, sat in a semicircle around Hunter as he conducted what he refers to as a have, do, are session. Everyone was dressed casually, including Hunter, who was clad in a green polo shirt, white pants, and tennis shoes. As the session unfolded, most of the participants dragged on cigarettes and sipped coffee from Styrofoam cups.

Half of the compulsive gamblers in the group were also recovering alcoholics or drug addicts, and four of them had attempted suicide prior to being admitted to treatment. One man had taken 100 Valium pills after gambling for several straight days, and one woman had been brought into the hospital by her family after overdosing on sleeping pills.

When Hunter announced the format of the session, one of the former patients, a sharp-witted brunette in her thirties, emitted a loud groan and said she was sick and tired of playing that game.

Hunter peered mischievously at the woman through his clear-framed glasses and laughed good-naturedly at the response. He then proceeded to coax out of the woman how she presently felt about herself. The woman described herself as "loving, worried, smart, sensitive, and fun," and then announced abruptly that she was "through playing." Hunter didn't press her further.

Hunter uses the have, do, are sessions to illustrate to the patients that the only area in which they have absolute responsibility and control is who they are, not what they have or do. "Outside random factors influence what you have or do," he tells the patients. "The one thing you should cherish above everything else is who you are. That's the only area in which you have complete control."

Afterward, Hunter noted that the patients generally

tend to emphasize what they have or do as a way of disavowing the "are" list because there are things on that list they don't like. He says the game is a simple self-discovery technique, but it usually produces positive results.

The November session seemed to validate Hunter's assessment. The tone of the session gradually evolved from negative to positive as everyone in the group shared one by one and gave feedback to one another. At the beginning of the session, one woman burst into tears as she talked about her prior gambling. "All I did was gamble and cry," she said.

Five people volunteered that they were self-centered; four said they were worried or nervous; and three noted that they were overly ambitious or competitive. Some of the self-judgments were particularly harsh. One current patient, who described himself as self-centered but caring, said he hated himself, and another man said he was self-centered, angry, and guilty and had lost track of who he was.

None of these responses seemed to faze Hunter, who slowly began to steer the patients to higher ground. He congratulated the group for their honesty and asked them to share how they had changed since coming into treatment.

A man from the Midwest who was being discharged from treatment the following day said he had been a basket case three weeks ago but he felt that he had a chance to build a new life with his wife and son when he returned home. He said he knew deep inside he was a loving person.

Hunter nodded with approval and focused on the young man who had said earlier that he hated himself. He too was being discharged from treatment the following day. The young man was what is known in the AA and GA communities as a "triple threat." He was an alcoholic and drug addict, as well as a compulsive gambler, and had been through drug treatment previously, but had relapsed. Hunter offered the young man some advice: "Go to meetings and take things one day at a time. Use the phone list from the meeting and talk to people. If you see people who need help, pick them up; they will do the same thing for you. Just remember you weren't ready to admit gambling was a problem when you came in here, so you've made a lot of progress."

CHANGING FEELINGS

Hunter asked members of the group to share their thoughts with the two men who were being discharged from treatment the next day.

One former patient, a housewife in her late thirties or early forties who had once contemplated suicide with a .357 magnum, told the young man, "Just think of gambling as a snake on our left shoulder. It's like a cobra waiting to strike."

She also offered advice to a man who was returning to his family in the Midwest. The man had said he was "confused and scared" and still filled with guilt. The woman said, "Sure, you've got a lot of guilt. I did, too. But remember to take a good look at what's gambling and what's not and go to meetings no matter how far away they are from your home."

The woman who had informed Hunter earlier that she was tired of playing the have, do, are game looked at the man from the Midwest squarely in the eye and said, "You've made the biggest change of anyone in this group. You've got a tendency to beat yourself up for what you did. You couldn't speak through the tears when you got here. You're going to be all right."

Hunter kept encouraging the group to share with the two men who were being discharged and after about twenty minutes, he began to bring the session to a close. He said enthusiastically, "That was a good show today. You're doing more than just changing your behavior. You are beginning to change how you feel about yourself."

He looked at the two men who were being discharged and said, "It's important to monitor your feelings. Don't let resentments build up; they snowball into self-dislike. I know you are uncomfortable about leaving and that you are already thinking three or four days ahead. Take things one day at a time and be careful, but enthusiastic."

After the session, Hunter retired to the staff lounge to return phone calls and to chat with Mary Lou Strachan, who had been in the group meeting. They talked about some particulars of her research with female gamblers. He told a visitor that he was proud of what Mary Lou has done, but said that he leaves research on compulsive gambling to others such as Jacobs, Lesieur, and Rosenthal. "The research is important, but all I'm interested in is the treatment end of compulsive gambling. It's not only rewarding, but at times, it's a lot of fun."

One of the participants in Dr. Rob Hunter's group was a trim, hip, thirty-two-year-old casino employee named Mark Catchings, who had checked himself into Charter Hospital of Las Vegas seven months earlier and hadn't gambled since. An alcoholic as well as compulsive gambler, Mark is a poker boss at the seven-card stud tables at one of the large casinos on the Las Vegas Strip. His present job is the third one he has held on the Strip. He was fired from his previous casino jobs as a result of drinking and gambling. "When I was on a gambling or drinking binge, I never showed up for work," he says. "I got four stacks of warning slips from one casino before they finally fired me."

WORKING TO RECOVER

Despite the fact that he is surrounded by gambling in his job, Mark hasn't been tempted to gamble since being discharged from the Charter program. "I see a lot of people playing who are exactly like I was," he says, "but so far, I haven't had an urge to play."

Dealers at the casino where he works are required to play poker in their off-duty hours at least once a week, but his bosses have waived that requirement for Mark. "I told my manager my whole story before I went to work there," he says, "and they've been very supportive. I wanted them and the other dealers I work with to know I'm a compulsive gambler. I think it helps me in my recovery."

Many casino workers in Las Vegas switch careers when they quit gambling, but for the present, Mark plans to stay in the business. "This is the only business I know," he says, "but if it becomes a problem, I'll quit."

To bolster his recovery, Mark participates in the one-year aftercare program at Charter Hospital and is a regular at GA meetings around town. He has a sponsor in GA and shares freely at the meetings he attends.

Mark says he was "partied down" when he was admitted to Charter Hospital on the fourth of July in 1989. More accurately, he was clinically depressed. He was mentally and physically exhausted and had begun holing up for a couple of days at a time in the bedroom of a house he shared with his girlfriend. He would draw the curtains, unplug the phone, lock the door and sleep virtually around the clock. His girlfriend said he was sponging and finally walked out on him. He says he "felt like crap" when he was admitted to the hospital but after a couple of days, he was ready to leave. He ended up staying three weeks and today he looks back on the experience as "good pain."

"It changed my life," he says. "I thought I was going to be the way I was my whole life. I thought gambling was what I did. I would tell any lie, anywhere, anytime, and say anything I wanted to get what I needed to gamble. I used people and wasn't nice to anyone. I was a perfect asshole. I told my girlfriend I was broke, but I kept $10,000 in $100 bills in a shoebox on a shelf in the top of my closet for gambling money.

"I discovered while I was in treatment that I was scared of people and had real low self-esteem. I didn't even think my own family loved me. I thought the only way I could be somebody was through gambling. I thought it was nice being known around town as a high roller. I'm getting rid of all that, and it feels good. I'm paying off all of my debts and getting honest with myself."

Mark also has quit drinking. He says he was always in trouble because of his drinking and never drew a sober breath for about four years after moving to Las Vegas from the Midwest in 1981 to land a job in a casino. Finally, though, he says his compulsive gambling overpowered his drinking. When he began gambling heavily, he cut down on his drinking so he would feel more in control.

After moving to Las Vegas, Mark got a job at a large hotel-casino where a friend worked. The friend, he says, was just like him—"a broken down, real piece of shit guy."

WINNING BIG

Mark, who had hung out around racetracks and played poker with his friends in his hometown in the Midwest, gambled compulsively from the moment he hit Las Vegas. "I loved action," he says. "I would see people win, and think, man, that's what I want—to win big. I was a real live one, always ramming and jamming, but I would hate myself when I lost and lose my temper and threaten anyone within earshot."

Mark says he made some big scores from time to time, but it was never enough. In the final year of his gambling, after he had been fired for the second time and had totalled his car, he would walk to the casinos and play video poker at the quarter and dollar machines for hours on end. He spent the rest of his time drinking beer and holing up in his bedroom.

He says it was a miserable existence, but the excitement of gambling sustained him. "I was always going for those $1,500 to $2,000 carousel jackpots, trying to get more money to gamble. I knew something was wrong with me, but I didn't know what to do about it except gamble some more. When I wasn't gambling, I was so sick I couldn't get out of bed."

Mark believes his recovery is a miracle and that it wouldn't have been possible without treatment. "I thought I would be a gambler and boozer until the day I died," he says. "My father was a gambler, and there is a lot of alcoholism in my family. I remember going to the racetrack with my father when I was a kid and sitting in the car waiting for him. I would sit there and cry when he stayed too long. My father was still gambling when he died at fifty-six."

Mark is optimistic now. "When I first got out of treatment, I dreamed about gambling every night," he says. "I haven't had a dream like that in about two months now, so I must be making progress. I'm beginning to slow down and feel at peace with myself for the first time in my life."

PROGRESS, NOT PERFECTION

Recovery from compulsive gambling is a daunting task: whether it's achieved through hospital treatment, private therapy, Gamblers Anonymous, a rare religious experience, or a combination thereof, it takes time and work. The act of stopping is usually not enough in and of itself to ensure continuing recovery from compulsive gambling. Compulsive gamblers must be willing—and able—to make fundamental changes in their behavior, their attitudes, and their life-styles. If they can't, they invariably return to gambling.

No one understands this better than Mike Brubaker, who has had to make some dramatic changes since laying down his last bet on a golf course in 1978. Changes aside, however, he still continues to struggle with some personality problems that predated his headlong plunge into alcoholism and compulsive gambling. These problems are known in GA and AA lingo as "character defects," and in Mike's mind the three defects he is still grappling with are impatience, intolerance, and a need to be in control.

"I've improved in all three of these areas," says Brubaker, "but I've still got a ways to go. When I become impatient, I get this big knot in my stomach. I'm learning to pay attention to that knot, and I'm asking myself questions about what caused it. As for intolerance, I'm short with my wife, Donna, on occasion and strike out at her verbally because she doesn't do things the way I think they ought to be done. We've been married three years, but I'm still learning how to be in a relationship.

"Most of my impatience and intolerance are caused by my need to be in control. I'm learning how to back off on things like organizing a second gamblers meeting in Monterey, or running everything in our marriage."

Mike's defects might not seem like big flaws to most people, but he is especially wary of reverting to his old ways. He regards recovery as a continual process and believes it would be nearly impossible to achieve it without a self-help program. A believer in a higher power, Mike has begun every morning for the past sixteen years "talking to God." He does this by reciting the Serenity Prayer, a basic tenet of the Twelve-Step programs ("God, grant me the serenity to accept the things I cannot change, courage to change the things I can, and wisdom to know the difference").

Mike's self-help program extends into a concern for others in recovery. He is a legend in self-help and treatment circles in California for keeping track of the sobriety dates (or "birthdays") for hundreds of people in alcohol and gambling groups. He maintains a list of birthdays in a file box and goes through the file on a monthly basis, transferring the names of people celebrating birthdays that month to a daily reminder calendar he carries with him at all times and a desktop calendar at work. Without fail, he sends birthday notes or cards to people in his file or calls them up on the telephone.

HELPING OTHERS

Len Baltzer, Mike's boss at Community Hospital Recovery Center in Monterey and his long-time mentor, marvels at

Mike's thoughtfulness. Baltzer says, "I can't imagine anyone taking the time to remember everyone's birthday. He
must spend $500 a year on cards and birthday items, not to
mention the phone calls."

Mike also has great enthusiasm for sponsoring people
on Twelve-Step programs for gambling and alcoholism. He
currently sponsors seven of the members at the Thursday
night compulsive gamblers meeting in Monterey and has
sponsored dozens of people recovering from alcoholism.

To encourage self-reliance on the part of former patients, Baltzer has a rule prohibiting members of the Community Hospital Recovery staff from sponsoring newly
discharged patients. "If I didn't have a rule," Baltzer says,
"Mike probably would want to sponsor half the people who
come through here. He gets very involved with the patients
and has confidence in his ability to help them."

Helping others with gambling or alcohol problems is
perhaps the key element of Mike Brubaker's recovery. Prior
to commencing his recovery, Mike, like most compulsive
gamblers, was extremely self-centered. Even though he was
never formally diagnosed, Mike met virtually every clinical
definition of a compulsive gambler. In addition to being
self-centered, he displayed a great number of the ancillary
and predisposing factors associated with compulsive gamblers. He felt unloved by his father and thought nothing he
did was ever good enough to please his father. He had low
self-esteem; he engaged in all-or-nothing thinking; he
thought money would solve all his problems; he feared intimacy; he resented authority; he had fantasies of power; he
needed to be in control to feel good about himself; and he
was dishonest, angry, competitive, restless, and intolerant.

His gambling habits themselves fit the classic pattern.
After he quit drinking, his gambling quickly progressed to
the point where he couldn't quit while he was ahead, and
he needed to play longer and bet bigger amounts to
achieve the level of excitement he desired. He also was pre-
occupied with gambling and had a total disregard for the

consequences of his gambling. The problems directly associated with his gambling disappeared in the first year of Mike's recovery. He found a sponsor, a recovering barber named Ted, and worked the Twelve Steps of the self-help recovery program, which included making a financial inventory and admitting to his family and others the extent of his gambling.

For that first year, Mike says, "The mere fact that I wasn't gambling was enough to sustain me."

Gradually, Mike began to work on making wrenching changes in other areas of his life. One of the most difficult was making peace with his father, who had developed full-blown alcoholism after retiring from the service station business in Tacoma, Washington, in 1980, the same year Mike retired from active duty in the Navy.

Mike visited his father shortly before Gerald Brubaker died of lung cancer and cirrhosis of the liver in 1982. "My father and I were able to resolve things between us," Mike says. "At first, he was angry with me for coming to see him. I hadn't visited him for a while because of his alcoholism. But I was able to talk to him a little and tell him that I loved him and that I wished we had been able to have a better relationship."

After his father died, Mike visited his mother's and father's graves one day and talked aloud about his feelings for them. "I sat there for about an hour, talking and crying," he says. Afterward, he felt much better; it was as if he had closed that chapter in his history.

FUN, FAMILY, AND RECOVERY

Mike's recovery from compulsive gambling was built on the foundation of the insights he had gained into himself during his treatment for alcoholism at the U.S. Navy Hospital in Long Beach and through his involvement in a Twelve-

Step alcoholism recovery program. He says those experiences helped make possible his recovery from compulsive gambling. He had obviously put some of the lessons he had learned in treatment on hold while he continued to gamble, but he says the feelings of dishonesty he was experiencing finally enabled him to break through the denial about his gambling problem.

"I finally realized that if I didn't get honest with myself, I was going to start drinking again," Mike says. "I was being dishonest about my finances and about the time the gambling was taking away from my family. I don't think I would have realized that when I did had it not been for my program of recovery for alcoholism. I didn't know the meaning of the word *honesty* while I was drinking."

Mike was able to use the same Twelve-Step principles to quit smoking on September 30, 1984, the tenth anniversary of the day he quit drinking. He admitted he was powerless over nicotine, just as he had admitted he was powerless over alcohol and gambling years earlier. Today, Mike can recite a long list of ways he has changed since he quit gambling in 1978. He says he is calmer and much more easygoing; friends are much more important to him now; he has more time for his children and grandchildren; he is more caring and concerned about what happens to other people; he is more considerate of others; he has enough self-esteem to say no; and he has more balance in his life for what he terms "fun, family, and recovery."

Mike adds with a laugh, however, that all of these changes are relative. "I was really out of control before I began my recovery, so I had a lot of room to improve."

Len Baltzer, a veteran alcoholism treatment administrator with twenty-two years of recovery from alcoholism, is in a unique position to gauge Mike Brubaker's progress. He was an alcoholism counselor at Long Beach Naval Hospital when Mike entered treatment there in 1974, and had no idea that Mike had a gambling problem until the two of them took their ill-fated golfing trip through Las Vegas. But even then, he had confidence that Mike could turn himself around.

Mike joined Baltzer in 1988 as a program supervisor in Monterey after working first as a counselor in the Navy and then at private treatment programs in San Pedro, Huntington Beach, Torrance, Bellflower, and Los Angeles.

Baltzer, a quiet, trim man with a deliberate manner of speaking, says that when he first met Mike Brubaker as a patient, he could have never imagined that Mike would one day become an alcoholism counselor. "I've met few people in my career who were as grandiose as Mike," Len says. "He embellished all of his accomplishments, and he embellished them a lot. It took him three or four weeks just to settle down. He had to have all the answers immediately, and had a lot of problem taking direction. His counselors had to sit him down and tell him to shut up and listen. He was a very difficult case."

LEARNING TO LISTEN

Mike still needs to "work on listening," Baltzer says. "You've got to listen to get information." But, he says, Mike has developed into a good counselor and is "much more teachable and has much more humility. His grandiosity will still peak from time to time. I tell him he will build up his own ego if nobody else will."

Baltzer was surprised when Mike applied for counselor training in the Navy in 1975. "I liked Mike, but I never pictured him as a counselor," Len says. "I thought all counselors had to have a great capacity to listen. But Mike proved me wrong. He is a fast learner and he learned to listen. He picked up the basics of counseling very quickly and then expanded upon those concepts.

"Mike has a very aggressive style of counseling, and it

helps him cut through the issues. His attitude is: the buck stops with me. His style won't work with everyone, but I think it's served Mike very well in dealing with people with special issues—such as celebrities, the wealthy, women, blacks, and gays. He always cuts straight to the heart of the problem."

Baltzer and Brubaker became friends on the golf course. "He started tagging along, and pretty soon he became a regular in our golfing group," Baltzer recalls. "Later Mike began to use golf as therapy for the people he was counseling and sponsoring. I remember Mike would bring Billy Carter along with us on the golf course while Billy was in treatment. Billy wasn't too interested in golf then, but I think he enjoyed getting out in the fresh air and looking for lost golf balls."

Baltzer says Mike has matured greatly during their fifteen-year friendship and that he has complete confidence in Mike. As a token of that confidence, Baltzer gives Brubaker a fairly free rein in working with compulsive gamblers undergoing alcohol or drug treatment in Monterey. "I know that gambling is a high priority with a lot of patients who come through here," Baltzer says, "but I'm not at all qualified to deal with it. Mike is, and I think it's great. He is concerned that gambling can lead to a relapse for our alcohol and drug patients, and he has a keen sense of the pitfalls facing gamblers. He talks about things that I would have never thought of. I believe he is doing a great service by working with gamblers."

Mike's wife, Donna, a realtor in Carmel, didn't know Mike when he was drinking or gambling, but she has noticed some major changes in Mike since she first met him in the early 1980s while she was working in a juvenile alcohol and drug diversion program that referred youngsters to San Pedro Peninsula Hospital where Mike worked as a counselor and supervisor.

Donna says Mike has matured noticeably since she first met him. When they were considering marriage, she took a long hard look at Mike's pluses and minuses before consenting. "I had been married before, and I didn't want to make a mistake," Donna says. "I knew Mike was a very controlling person, but what concerned me more was his maturity. But when I looked closely at him, I could see he was much more understanding and more tolerant than when I first met him and that his moods were much more steady. Anyway, the good points far outweighed the bad, and Mike has given 100 percent to our marriage, just like he does to everything else."

Donna says she was familiar with recovery from alcoholism and drug dependency through her former career in the field, but she knew little about compulsive gambling until she and Mike were married. "We talk about compulsive gambling at times," Donna says, "and I think I've learned to appreciate how difficult recovery is. I like to buy a lottery ticket from time to time and participate in raffles, but I know Mike can't do that, no matter how harmless it might seem."

MONEY MATTERS

She has also taken note of Mike's ambivalence about money and financial matters. On one hand, she says Mike is very generous ("He's always slipping the kids twenty or fifty dollars, or giving somebody in need a few dollars"), but on the other hand, he's very skittish about carrying too much cash or about not paying bills the moment they arrive in the mail.

Donna says that unfortunately, she is not a whiz at managing money, and she hopes that someday she and Mike will be able to hire someone to manage their finances to relieve Mike of that burden. "It just doesn't seem fair for Mike, a gambling addict, to have to worry about managing money," she says.

The only other remnant of Mike's gambling personality that Donna has observed is his competitiveness at cards and board games such as Monopoly and Trivial Pursuit. "I think one of the biggest fights we've had since we got married was over a board game," she says. "Mike got furious when things didn't go his way. Finally, we agreed to never play again."

Donna says she tries to be supportive of Mike in his work with recovering gamblers and alcoholics. "I know that's very important to his recovery," she says, "but sometimes he'll just go until he collapses. I tell him that he's got to learn to say no more often, and he has improved some. I think he concentrates on gamblers because he knows how difficult recovery is, and he knows that a lot of them have absolutely no resources. Mike is really just a great big teddy bear. He treats my children just like his own, and he is friendly and kind to everyone. I think he's finally found some serenity for himself."

One of the most trying periods in Mike Brubaker's recovery was the end of his twenty-six-year marriage to Marjorie Brubaker. The couple was divorced in 1986 after several periods of separation. Mike wanted the divorce; Marjorie did not.

Mike was unhappy in the marriage and says "I didn't want to spend the rest of my life with someone I didn't love." He says both Marjorie and he probably stayed together for the wrong reasons early in their marriage, as do many couples involved in alcoholic marriages.

"In the middle of my alcohol and gambling addiction, I wanted someone who would be there for me," Mike says, "and Marjorie was the type of person who needed to take care of someone. I think she thought if she took care of me, lied for me, and pretty much ignored or forgave my addictions, she would get me sober and everything would be all right. Neither one of us had any self-esteem. I think the only time either of us was truly happy was at work."

A CHANCE TO BE HAPPY

Mike and Marjorie's marriage seemed to improve in the early part of Mike's sobriety, but he attributes that primarily to the fact that the two of them and their two children were together as a family for the first time. After the children, Patrick and Emily, were grown and Mike settled into a regular job close to home, he began to realize that he and Marjorie didn't have much in common. Mike had spent most of their married life on overseas duty in the Navy. In fact, he left for a year overseas immediately after they were married in 1960, and when he returned to Seattle for his first extended shore duty, the couple separated for a period because of Mike's drinking.

"When things settled down in Long Beach after the children were grown," Mike says, "Marjorie and I found out we didn't communicate very well and that we really didn't know each other. We tried counseling, retreats, and a couple of trial separations, but nothing worked. I was unhappy in our marriage and thought I deserved a chance to be happy. It wasn't Marjorie's fault."

Mike says he gave Marjorie what she asked for in their divorce settlement. "I thought she deserved it for all the crap she put up with when I was drinking and gambling," he says. "She is a good mother and did a good job of raising our kids when I wasn't there."

Mike Brubaker occasionally has pangs of regret that he can't participate in even the most innocent forms of gambling, such as raffles or Monte Carlo nights for fund-raisers. He also has gone as far as to fantasize about making a bet in Las Vegas. But when he finds himself drifting, Mike relies on the second step of his Twelve-Step Program to get back on course. The step says, "[We] came to believe that a power greater than ourselves could restore us to a normal way of thinking and living."

He says that when he's thinking rationally, he realizes

that a win at even the simplest game of chance—like a fast food rub-off card—could set him off. "I always try to think through what would happen if I won anything. My mind would start racing, and before I knew it, I would be off and running. I have to keep reminding myself that even when I won, I lost because winning always led to more gambling."

Mike says early on in his recovery from compulsive gambling he read an article that said only 2 percent of all compulsive gamblers ever recover. "I decided I wanted to be in that 2 percent, and that in time, maybe I could help raise that percentage a little by helping others."

Easter Week of 1990 wasn't one of Mike Brubaker's better weeks. He started the week by dressing himself in a hot, uncomfortable and ridiculous Easter Bunny costume for a fund-raiser that his wife organized. Later, he quite unaccountably broke his wrist swinging a golf club. Then on Easter Sunday, he came down with a bad cold after traveling from Monterey to San Diego to help a friend celebrate his fifteenth AA birthday.

By Wednesday of the following week, however, he was back on track. He had received encouraging news about funding for a series of compulsive gambling videos he was working on with a producer in Los Angeles, and the second self-help meeting for compulsive gamblers in Monterey was beginning to take shape. He had even begun to regard the broken wrist as a blessing in disguise because he reasoned that since it would prevent him from playing golf he would have more time to study for the final of a psychology course with which he was struggling.

Michael Brubaker was off and running again, and this time the odds were decidedly in his favor.

RESOURCES

The National Council on
  Problem Gambling, Inc.
445 West 59th Street
New York, NY 10019
(212) 765-3833
(800) 522-4700

California Council on
  Compulsive Gambling
435 North Roxbury Drive
Beverly Hills, CA 90210
(408) TRY-9099
(800) FACTS-4-U (in California
  only)

Canadian Foundation on Compulsive Gambling (Ontario)
505 Consumers Road, Suite 605
Willowdale, Ontario M2J 4V8
Canada
(416) 499-9800 (business hours)
(416) 222-7477 (after hours)

Connecticut Council on
  Compulsive Gambling
P.O. Box 6244
Hamden, CT 06517
(203) 453-1729

Delaware Council on Gambling
  Problems, Inc.
113 West 8th Street
Wilmington, DE 19801
(302) 655-3261

Florida Council on Compulsive
  Gambling, Inc.
P.O. Box 947664

Maitland, FL 32794-7664
(407) 875-2425
(800) 432-5241 (nationwide hot
  line)

The Council on Compulsive
  Gambling of Illinois, Inc.
3535 North Odell Avenue
Chicago, IL 60634
(312) 889-0015

Maryland Council on
  Compulsive Gambling, Inc.
657 Gairloch Place
Belair, MD 21014
(301) 879-8460

Massachusetts Council on
  Compulsive Gambling
190 High Street, Suite 6
Boston, MA 02110
(617) 426-4554
(800) 822-7773 (in Massachusetts only)

Minnesota Council on
  Compulsive Gambling
702 Torrey Building
314 West Superior Street
Duluth, MN 55802
(218) 722-1503

Nevada Council on Compulsive
  Gambling, Inc.
4535 West Sahara Street,
  Suite 112-H
Las Vegas, NV 89102
(702) 364-2625
(800) 729-GAMB (nationwide)

*Council on Compulsive
   Gambling of New Jersey*
1315 West State Street
Trenton, NJ 08618
(609) 500-3299
(800) GAMBLER (nationwide)

*Council on Problem and
   Compulsive Gambling of
   North Dakota*
P.O. Box 10292
Fargo, ND 58107
(701) 293-1887

*Ohio Council on Problem
   Gambling*
P.O. Box 41262
Brecksville, OH 44141
(800) 457-7117 (in Ohio only)
(216) 585-4162

*Council on Compulsive
   Gambling of Pennsylvania*
P.O. Box 643
Lafayette Hill, PA 19444
(215) 744-1880

*Washington State Council on
   Problem Gambling*
P.O. Box 898
Lynnwood, WA 98046
(206) 527-0146

*Institute for the Study of
   Gambling and Commercial
   Gaming*
University of Nevada, Reno
Reno, NV 89557-0016
(702) 784-1477

Gam-Anon
P.O. Box 157
Whitestone, NY 11357
(718) 352-1671

*National Self-Help
   Clearinghouse*
25 West 43rd Street
Suite 620
New York, NY 10036
(212) 642-2944

*Institute of Certified Financial
   Planners*
Two Denver Highlands
10065 East Harvard Avenue,
   Suite 320
Denver, CO 80231
(303) 751-7600

*International Association of
   Financial Planners*
Two Concourse Parkway,
   Suite 800
Atlanta, GA 30328
(404) 395-1605

*Gamblers Anonymous
   International Service Office*
P.O. Box 17173
Los Angeles, CA 90017
(213) 386-8789

*National Clearinghouse for
   Alcohol and Drug Information*
P.O. Box 2345
Rockville, MD 20852
(301) 468-2600

LOCAL OFFICES OF
GAMBLERS ANONYMOUS

ARIZONA
- Phoenix: (602) 582-2089

CALIFORNIA
- Los Angeles: (213) 260-4657
- Sacramento: (916) 447-5588
- San Diego: (619) 239-2911
- San Francisco: (800) 541-7867
- San Jose: (800) 541-7867

CANADA
- Calgary: (403) 237-0654
- Montreal: (514) 484-6666
- Toronto: (416) 366-7613
- Vancouver: (604) 685-5510

CONNECTICUT
- statewide: (203) 777-5585

FLORIDA
- Miami: (305) 447-2696

GEORGIA
- Atlanta: (404) 237-7281

ILLINOIS
- Chicago: (312) 346-1588

LOUISIANA
- New Orleans: (504) 836-4543

MASSACHUSETTS
- Boston: (617) 642-8321
- Springfield: (413) 732-7854

MICHIGAN
- statewide: (313) 446-5144

MINNESOTA
- Minneapolis: (612) 922-3956

Missouri
- St. Louis: (314) 647-1111

Nebraska
- Omaha: (402) 978-7557

Nevada
- Las Vegas: (702) 385-7735, (702) 459-0864

New Jersey
- statewide: (201) 756-1171

New York
- Long Island: (516) 586-7171
- New York City: (212) 265-8600
- Syracuse: (315) 458-0085

Ohio
- Cincinnati: (513) 244-9779
- Cleveland: (216) 771-2248
- Toledo: (419) 245-0173

Oklahoma
- Oklahoma City: (405) 525-2026

Oregon
- Portland: (503) 233-5888

Pennsylvania
- Philadelphia: (215) 468-1991
- Pittsburgh: (412) 281-7484

Tennessee
- Knoxville: (615) 588-4755
- Nashville: (615) 254-6454

Texas
- Dallas: (214) 634-2095
- Houston: (713) 684-6654

Washington
- Seattle: (206) 464-9514

West Virginia
- Wheeling: (304) 234-8161

INDEX